"*A bend in the road is not the end of the road...unless you fail to make the turn.*"

—HELEN KELLER

Under the Apple Tree
As Time Goes By
We'll Meet Again
Till Then
I'll Be Seeing You
Fools Rush In
Let It Snow
Accentuate the Positive
For Sentimental Reasons
That's My Baby
A String of Pearls
Somewhere Over the Rainbow
Down Forget-Me-Not Lane
Set the World on Fire

Set the World on Fire

Beth Adams

Scripture references are from the following sources: *The Holy Bible, King James Version* (KJV). *The Holy Bible, New International Version* (NIV). Copyright © 1973, 1978, 1984, 2011 by Biblica, Inc. Used by permission of Zondervan. All rights reserved worldwide. www.zondervan.com.

Cover and interior design by Müllerhaus
Cover illustration by Greg Copeland at Illustration Online LLC.
Typeset by Aptara, Inc.

ISBN 978-1-961126-76-3 (hardcover)
ISBN 978-1-961126-77-0 (epub)

Printed and bound in the United States of America
10 9 8 7 6 5 4 3 2 1

SET THE WORLD ON FIRE

CHAPTER ONE

The lunch crowd finally started to clear out. Janet Shaw stood behind the register and rang up the bill for one of the last tables. Tuesdays weren't usually this busy, and while Janet was grateful for the business, she was ready to pack it in. Paulette Connor—who helped out in the dining room most days—had already left, since they were half an hour past their normal closing time.

"I'll watch for your booth at the fair," Janet said to the departing customers, waving to them as they walked toward the door.

The older couple had told her that they were in town for the homecoming festival—officially the American Soldiers Homecoming Tribute Festival—that Kim Smith had arranged at the Dennison Railroad Depot Museum. Volunteers at the Dennison Depot had famously welcomed and fed soldiers passing through on their way to and coming home from World War II, and the little town had a reputation for honoring the soldiers who had fought for their country. Kim, who ran the museum, had arranged the festival to celebrate the local veterans, as well as to attract some attention to the museum and its newly refurbished Pullman car, which could be rented out to stay in overnight.

Janet had been chatting with the couple and learned that they made military-themed T-shirts and sweatshirts, which they would sell from a booth at the festival. "I hope you sell a lot," Janet said.

"Thank you," the woman responded. "We'll be looking for you."

Janet waved, and they walked out.

Her best friend and business partner, Debbie Albright, emerged from the kitchen with a bucket of soapy water in her hands.

"This bodes well for the homecoming festival," Debbie said. "It doesn't even start for a few days, and there are already so many new people in town." She dunked a dishcloth in the bucket and started to wipe down the counter.

"It's great," Janet said. "I'm so happy for Kim. It'll be really good for the museum."

"It's not going to be bad for us either," Debbie said. "As long as we can keep up."

"We'll manage fine. We always do."

Janet glanced over at the table occupied by Austin and Carrie Wilson, fellow members of Faith Community Church and old friends. She didn't want to rush them, especially as they seemed to be in some kind of deep discussion. She would work on cleaning the rest of the dining room, and perhaps by the time she had everything else done, they'd be ready to go. She took another dishcloth and started wiping the tables and straightening chairs.

When she came to the corner table, she spotted something on the floor underneath it. Janet bent down, tugged it free, and saw it was a receipt.

New Philadelphia Military Surplus Store, it said at the top. Dated that morning. Someone had bought a glass bottle, gloves, some rope, a knife, a few T-shirts—all kinds of random things, apparently.

She tried to remember who'd been sitting at this table. Possibly that man who dealt in antique firearms. He was also here for the festival and planned to set up a booth to sell his historic weapons. Collectible Winchester repeating rifles and such, he'd told her. She didn't know if he'd need this receipt, but it must have fallen out of the black duffel bag he'd had with him. She'd keep it in case he came back for it. She folded the receipt, tucked it in her pocket, and kept cleaning the dining room.

Finally, when the Wilsons' table was the last one left to clean, Carrie raised her head and seemed to realize for the first time that they were alone.

"I'm so sorry, Janet." Carrie pushed herself up, and Austin reluctantly stood as well. "I didn't realize how late it had gotten."

"That's all right," Janet said. "Did you enjoy your meal?"

"It was delicious, as always," Austin said. He was tall and broad-shouldered, a vestige of his former career as a Marine. These days, Austin was a pediatric nurse at the hospital who sometimes played the trumpet in the community band. He was heading up a clothing drive to help needy veterans as part of the festival. He and Carrie had come in for lunch after a meeting with Kim Smith.

"I'm so glad," Janet said. "I don't want to rush you, but I can ring you up whenever you're ready."

"We're ready." Carrie finished her lemonade and set the glass on the table. "I'm sorry we took so long. We got talking and lost track of time."

"No worries whatsoever. Thank you for the project you've taken on for this weekend. It's a great cause."

"We hope it helps," Carrie said. "There are so many veterans in need."

"Ian went through his closet, so I have a bunch of clothes to donate," Janet said. Her husband had needed to clean out his closet for a while, truthfully, and this was a good excuse.

"Feel free to bring them by our place before the festival," Carrie said. "It's all coming back to our place anyway, and we'll have limited space in the car, so we may need to make several trips. If you brought your donation to us ahead of time, you'd likely save us a trip."

"No problem. I'll bring it over to you sometime this week," Janet said.

"Thank you so much." Carrie hoisted her purse onto her shoulder, and she and Austin walked to the register, where Debbie waited to ring them up. Debbie punched the buttons on the register for their meal, and Carrie grabbed a pack of Black Jack gum and a package of Necco wafers from the display of nostalgic candy they had for the festival. "We'll take these too," Carrie said. "Tyler loves this stuff."

"Better add some of that peanut candy," Austin said.

"I didn't see that. He is a fiend about it." Carrie grabbed another package and set them all on the counter.

"How is Tyler?" Janet asked as Debbie added the candy to their total.

"He's doing as well as can be expected," Carrie said. "He's struggling, but he's doing all right, I suppose."

Tyler, Carrie and Austin's son, had been a baseball star at the high school. He'd won sponsorships, had been recruited for travel teams, and even played in the High School World Series. He'd gone off to Ohio State on a baseball scholarship three years ago. But an injury early in the season his sophomore year had blown out his knee, requiring surgery, and the physical therapy had taken longer than expected. He'd eventually lost his scholarship and his sponsorship and had to come home. "He's working on getting back into shape, and we're hoping to find another school for him."

"I'll be praying for him," Janet said as Debbie swiped Austin's credit card. "I bet once he's fully recovered and playing, colleges will be fighting over him."

"I hope so, but mostly we hope he gets through this rough patch okay," Austin said.

"It can be really hard at this age," Janet said. Her own daughter, Tiffany, was two years younger than Tyler, and though Tiffany was doing well and enjoying being home for the summer, Janet knew she had her moments. It could be so hard to find one's footing at her age. "But Tyler's a good kid. He'll get through this."

"Thank you, Janet." Carrie tucked the candy and gum into her purse, and then she and Austin said goodbye and walked out.

Debbie began pulling the leftover pastries out of the display case. "What was that about?"

Debbie had gotten acquainted with Carrie and Austin at church, but she probably didn't know Tyler. She had moved back to Dennison just over a year ago, when Tyler's success and subsequent fall from stardom wasn't news anymore.

"Their son, Tyler, is a baseball star, but since he had an injury and lost his scholarship, he's been having a hard time and getting into some trouble. He had a bad car accident a few weeks ago. Ian told me about it when he came home and said Tyler was lucky to be alive. I got the impression that alcohol was involved, though of course Ian didn't come out and say that."

"I'm glad he's okay," Debbie said. "No one else was hurt?"

"No, thankfully," Janet said. She locked the door then cleaned the last table. "In any case, he seems to be recovering from his knee surgery and getting back into baseball, so maybe he'll do better soon."

"Let's hope so." Debbie put the leftover pastries away, and together they finished cleaning the dining room. "See you bright and early," she said as they walked out to the parking lot.

"Enjoy your afternoon." Janet headed to her car and drove through the charming streets of Dennison.

The small town was pretty in all seasons, but in July the roses and hydrangeas were in full bloom, the leafy green oaks and plane trees shaded the streets, and the whole town seemed to burst with life and excitement. The downtown area was busy this afternoon, no doubt due to the people in town for the festival. It was going to be a busy week.

Janet swung by the grocery store on her way home. Once she got home and had unpacked everything in her kitchen, she put together a cold sesame noodle salad she planned to take to church that night. Pastor Nick was leading a Bible study on the book of Ruth, and everyone was encouraged to bring a dish to share. Janet looked forward to the lesson.

Ian came home from the police station in time for them to drive to the church together, and they enjoyed the potluck dinner and fellowship before Pastor Nick started explaining about the culture and history of the Israelites in the time of Ruth. By the time they were headed home, Janet was pleasantly full and sleepily mulling over the fascinating discussion. She relaxed in the passenger seat while Ian drove through the quiet streets.

She didn't really register the first siren. She vaguely heard the low whining sound but didn't think anything of it until Ian's phone rang. Janet glanced down at the phone resting on the console between their seats. *Mike Gleason*, it said on the screen. The head of the fire department. If he was calling Ian after work hours, it was probably important.

"It's the fire chief," she said. "Do you want me to answer it?"

"Sure," Ian said, nodding. "Thanks."

"Hi, Mike, this is Janet," she said. "Ian is driving."

"Hi, Janet." Mike Gleason was originally from Boston and had a thick accent, despite having spent the past several decades in Ohio. "Can you relay a message to him? Something big has come up."

A second siren came screaming up behind them, and Ian pulled over to the side of the road to let the oncoming fire truck pass.

"Sure. Where do you need him?" she asked over the noise. Ian was the chief of police for the small town of Dennison, and she was used to him being summoned to anything big that happened in town.

"Over at the warehouse on Stillwater. There's a fire."

Janet passed the message on to Ian.

"Tell him I'm on my way," Ian said. He pulled back onto the road and followed the fire truck.

"He's on his way," Janet said into the phone. "We'll be there soon."

"Great. Thanks." The line went dead. Janet's first thought was that someone had been shooting off leftover fireworks and had sparked a fire. But she could see by the set of Ian's mouth that he was concerned.

"Are you familiar with this warehouse?" Janet vaguely knew where the row of warehouses was, on an industrial street on the outskirts of town.

"That's a municipal storage facility," Ian said. He pressed his foot down on the gas pedal. They were definitely over the speed limit, but the police chief wasn't likely to get a speeding ticket while responding to an emergency. "Lots of different departments store things there. The police department uses it to store crime-scene evidence."

"Does that mean—"

"It's where we store the evidence for all the crimes that have been committed in our area and for cases that are awaiting trial," Ian said grimly. "If it's on fire, that's a very bad thing."

CHAPTER TWO

Janet grimly held on as Ian sped toward the warehouse, following the route the fire truck had taken out of downtown Dennison. Her mind spun. If the evidence burned, what would that mean for those cases when they went to trial? Would the trials be fair, if they could be held at all? Would criminals walk free? And what about the other departments in town that had things stored in the warehouse?

She couldn't ask Ian about all that now, as he was focused on getting to the warehouse quickly. She hoped he remembered he was driving his personal car, not a police cruiser with sirens, but she held her tongue. She grabbed for the door handle as he whipped onto Stillwater and the plumes of thick dark smoke became visible against the deepening summer sky.

Already a dozen or so cars were parked along the road as they neared the warehouse. Ian drove as close as he could before pulling into an open spot and exiting the car. Janet could see the flames leaping into the sky from where she was sitting. She hesitated, then climbed out of the car.

Firefighters—most of them volunteers pulled from their summer evening plans—sprayed the fire with water from the hoses, but it didn't seem to be doing much good. Burt Margolies worked at the pumper truck, but the water evaporated as it soon as it hit the hot air. Greg Connor held the hose steady anyway. Thick, heavy smoke hung in clouds around him.

Janet moved closer, trying to see where Ian had gone, but a uniformed police officer stepped forward, arms out. His name bar said MEYERS. He was the newest member of the team, who had joined the force a few months ago. She also saw Deputy Brendan Vaughn trying to control the crowd.

"Stay back," Meyers told her, not unkindly.

She could see now that she was one of several people trying to get closer to the fire. She recognized Barry Smith and Mark Thomas, and there were also several people she didn't know.

"I need you all to stay back so the firefighters can do their job," Meyers said.

Janet pulled out her phone and sent a quick text to Tiffany. YOUR DAD GOT A CALL HE HAD TO DEAL WITH. WE'LL BE HOME AS SOON AS WE CAN.

NO PROBLEM. THANKS FOR LETTING ME KNOW, Tiffany texted back. She had a summer job as a lifeguard at the local pool and usually came home exhausted from long days in the sun, but she often went out with friends in the evening. Whatever she was up to, at least now she wouldn't worry.

The heat from the flames radiated from the building, but it was the noise that surprised Janet the most. The roar of the flames was almost deafening, and the scene was cast in an eerie orange glow. Mike Gleason shouted to be heard over the fire, directing the firefighters as they struggled to aim the water at the base of the flames.

A shower of sparks flew up as part of the roof caved in, and Janet stepped back, as did several of the other spectators around her.

Ian spoke to Mike, who pointed toward the west side of the warehouse. Another car rushed up, and Janet recognized local reporter Jim Watson, who jumped out of his car, camera and notebook in hand.

Janet wanted to help, but she didn't know what to do, so she did the only thing she could think of. *Please, Lord, help them put that fire out quickly,* she prayed. *Please keep the firefighters safe and protect whatever's inside.*

More and more volunteer firefighters arrived and joined the fight, lining up along hoses in their protective gear. Janet didn't know how much time had passed, but little by little the flames were lower in the sky, and the sound of the fire lessened. Finally, the smoke changed from a thick black plume to lighter gray. The flames died down, and the fire seemed to be under some semblance of control. It was still another half hour or so before the firefighters began coiling up the hoses and returning the protective gear to the trucks so they could head for home.

Ian was deep in conversation with several other police officers as well as Mike. Janet didn't want to interrupt, but she was getting tired of standing around. The onlookers started to get back in their cars and leave. Jim Watson waited off to one side, no doubt hoping to speak to Ian or the fire chief.

Eventually, Ian's conversation wrapped up, and he made his way to Janet. "I'm sorry. It looks like I'm going to be here a while. Why don't you head home? I'll catch a ride when I'm done here."

"Did it all burn?" Janet asked. "Were they able to save anything?"

"It's too early to tell," Ian said with a sigh. "We won't know that until we can get in there, and Mike says it's not safe to go in yet."

"Do they know how it started?" Janet asked. A gnawing suspicion had begun as she'd stood watching the fire burn. Buildings could catch on fire for all kinds of reasons—bad electrical work, grease on a cooking flame, a dropped cigarette that hadn't been properly extinguished, overloaded circuits, fireworks gone awry. But if part of this building was used for police evidence storage, was there a chance that it hadn't been an accident?

"Mike has some theories," Ian said.

"Was it set on purpose?" Janet pressed.

"We're pretty sure it wasn't an accident. According to Mike, someone probably used an accelerant, maybe gasoline, to get the flames to catch faster. But we'll know more after he's had a chance to investigate."

"Do you think someone set it to destroy police evidence?" Janet asked.

"It's possible. We can't say yet. We'll investigate where in the warehouse the fire started and how it was set. Obviously, there's a lot to sort through here, and we have to wait for the state fire marshal. It's going to be a while. You go on home, and I'll get there as soon as I can."

Janet hesitated. She hated to leave him without a ride home. But several police cars were on-site. Someone would bring him home when he was ready.

"All right," she said. "Is there anything you need?"

"No." Ian shook his head. "I'll be fine."

"Okay," Janet said. "I'll see you at home."

"It could be a while." Ian leaned in for a kiss. "Don't wait up."

"Okay. I love you. Be safe." Janet kissed his cheek then headed back to the car.

When she got in the car, she gaped at the clock on the dash. It was later than she had thought. She took one last glance at the shell of the warehouse—all blackened steel and twisted corrugated metal—before she drove off, her headlights sweeping across the road as she made a U-turn. The streets of downtown Dennison seemed so quiet after the noise and chaos of the fire. After a few minutes she pulled into her driveway and parked beside Tiffany's little car. The lights in the living room were on.

Janet climbed out of the car and walked into the house. "Hi, Tiffany." She set her purse on the bench by the door and kicked off her shoes. "How was your night?"

"Okay." Tiffany sat on the couch, her feet propped on the coffee table and her phone in her hand. She was tanned and had let her dark-red hair grow out during her freshman year, so now it spilled over her shoulders. She wore cutoff shorts and a sweatshirt that said CASE WESTERN TENNIS. "How about you? Everything okay with Dad?"

"There was a fire at a warehouse the police use to store evidence," Janet said. "And it seems like it may have been intentional. He stayed behind to investigate."

"Wow." Tiffany raised her eyebrows. "So which of the perps he was about to put away set the fire? You know it had to be one of them."

"I think that's a possibility, though they won't know anything for sure until their investigation is complete," Janet said. "For now, it's past my bedtime."

"Cool. I'm going to go meet Layla and Hudson."

"All right. Have fun. And text if you're going to be really late. Be safe." She said that even though Tiffany had been living on her own at school and didn't need her mother nagging her. Old habits died hard.

"I will." Tiffany walked to the door, grabbed her bag, tucked her phone into her back pocket, and opened the door. "By the way, a bunch of us are planning to go to Hudson's cousin's cabin for a weekend soon."

"Is that the same one you've talked about before?"

Tiffany nodded. "Yeah."

"Don't forget we're leaving for vacation a week from Friday." A week and a half from now, the three of them would stay in a rented cabin on a lake they'd gone to for many years.

"We're thinking about the weekend after that. We're coming back from vacation on Friday, right? We'd go up to Hudson's cousin's place the next day."

"Okay." Janet considered this. "Where is the cabin exactly?"

"I don't know. Hudson said it's about an hour away. It's on a lake."

"Who all's going?"

"Layla and Hudson, and Hudson's friend Liam. Plus maybe Hudson's sister. She just graduated from Case Western."

"Okay." Though Janet's mom brain immediately started going through all the trouble they could get into, she wasn't about to tell Tiffany not to go, as much as she wanted to. Her daughter was an adult now, and she handled herself well. "You don't have to work?"

"Jamie said he'd switch a couple of days with me," Tiffany said.

"Okay. Well, keep me posted."

"All right. Have a good night."

"My bed is already calling to me. I'll see you tomorrow."

Janet watched her go. Everything was different now, after less than a year apart. Tiffany had grown up so much in that time, and she'd come back with all kinds of habits and ideas that Janet hadn't been prepared for. She knew it was good and developmentally appropriate. But still, she sometimes struggled with how to navigate the changes and often missed those days when Tiffany needed her more.

Janet watched as the headlights of her daughter's car vanished from the driveway, and then she headed up to the bedroom and got ready for bed. She showered off the smell of the smoke, climbed into bed, and fell asleep as soon as her head hit the pillow.

Janet woke to the beeping of her alarm and winced as she rolled over. How was it time to get up already?

Ian was asleep beside her and didn't even stir. She stumbled out of bed and downstairs to the kitchen to get the coffee started. Tiffany's bag was in the foyer, and her car was in the driveway. She'd made it home. Ian had dropped a folder of papers and a notebook on the kitchen table before he'd gone to bed. The cover of the notebook had flopped open, and the papers were in disarray. He must have been exhausted.

The edges of the sky were just starting to lighten. Debbie had said many times how much she would hate getting up as early as Janet had to, but Janet liked the quiet of the early mornings. As she got dressed for work, it felt as if she were the only one awake in the world, and she enjoyed the undistracted time to pray and think about the day ahead.

She finished her coffee and set her mug in the sink. She started toward the door but paused when her gaze caught on something in Ian's open notebook. It was a note written in Ian's scrawling cursive, but she didn't have any trouble making out the words.

At first, she couldn't make sense of it, but then she began to understand what it was.

Well, this is interesting.

CHAPTER THREE

Dennison, Ohio
1959

John scanned the church basement, crowded with men and women in their Sunday best. Grandma wore her favorite yellow dress. She'd added the lace so cleverly you almost couldn't see the rip at the hem, and she'd added some new feathers to her tired old hat.

Grandpa had on his suit—his only suit. Daddy had one too. He'd gotten it when Uncle Robert got sick and lost all that weight, so it didn't fit him anymore. John's own suit was three sizes too small, his pant legs finishing two inches above his ankles. Mama said they couldn't afford to get him a new one this year.

Gazing around the crowded room, all he saw was people making do. Wearing things until they gave out altogether. Struggling to make ends meet. Sure, they

were laughing, talking, catching up. Fellowshipping.
Here in this church basement, no one seemed to mind
that none of them had enough. That they couldn't get
jobs that would pay what they were worth. That they
were janitors, porters, and maids instead of doctors,
lawyers, and business owners.

But not him. He wouldn't settle for this kind of
life. He didn't see how they could either. One way or
another, he was getting out of here as soon as he could.
And he would never look back.

Janet read the list of names Ian had written in his notebook and realized it was a list of potential suspects for the fire at the warehouse.

Ward—gas can, lighter, section of wall where fire started
Wilson—beer cans, car, photographs on thumb drive
Mills—upholstery, electrical panel, photographs on thumb drive
Merrick—Springfield Trapdoor 1873

The items after their names were probably evidence from their cases that had been stored in the warehouse. Ian must have been tired since he'd left something like this out in the open. He was usually so meticulous about keeping his work classified.

Wilson was likely Tyler Wilson, Austin and Carrie's son. She scanned the rest of the names. Judging by what she saw, she guessed Mills might be Todd Mills, a contractor who had done work for the depot museum, but she couldn't be sure. She didn't know the other names, though she guessed Ward, whoever that was, had been arrested for arson, judging by the list of items in evidence. Someone who had been previously arrested for arson would be a likely suspect in this case.

Then again, it was a shared warehouse. Something stored by one of the other departments could have been the reason for the fire. Though it was hard to imagine that the parks and rec department or the sanitation department would have anything in the warehouse worth committing arson for. Still, it was possible.

Janet shook herself. She needed to get going. She was responsible for all the goodies they sold at the Whistle Stop Café, and they wouldn't bake themselves. She filled food bowls for Ranger the cat and Laddie the Yorkshire terrier, and then she went out to the car. The streets were empty, and the sky was still dark as she drove to the Whistle Stop.

Inside the kitchen at the café, Janet put an apron on over her jeans and T-shirt and got started on the day's scones, peaches and cream. She mixed the dry ingredients in one bowl, the wet ones in another, and then stirred them together. She turned the dough out onto the cutting board and shaped it. Scones were versatile and meditative to make, which was why she loved them. As she worked, her mind kept flashing back to the fire last night, to the smoke and the flames and the sound.

There was a family she knew from church whose house had caught fire a few years ago, sparked by a coffee maker someone forgot to turn off. They'd lost everything—clothing, furniture, the children's toys, treasured photo albums and mementos—and had to rely on their community for food, clothing, and housing until the insurance money came through. It had been tragic, though they repeatedly said they were grateful no one was hurt and that so many people supported them.

Any time a building burned, the things inside were damaged, if not by the fire itself, then by the water and smoke. In this case, what had been damaged was not replaceable things like furniture and clothing, but evidence that would help to put criminals behind bars. How much evidence had been destroyed? And how much would it matter to those cases? If Ian didn't figure out who had done this, would the public pay the price?

She cut the scones, slid them into the oven, and then moved on to mixing the ingredients for blueberry muffins. She tried to focus her mind on the task at hand, but she couldn't stop thinking about the fire. She was grateful when Debbie came in.

"Good morning," her friend called.

"Good morning. How are you?" Janet dropped a spoonful of batter into a muffin cup.

"I'm all right. How are you? I heard about the fire at the warehouse last night." Debbie put her bag down and moved to the sink to wash her hands.

"We were on the way home from Bible study when Ian got the call, so I was there. It was pretty intense." Janet filled her friend in on the fire as she finished scooping muffins and slid them into the oven.

When she was done, Debbie shook her head. "I sure hope they find whoever did this. If there's a chance someone set that fire to get rid of the evidence of their crime, that's a really big deal."

"I think there were only four cases with evidence in the warehouse, so hopefully the police don't have too many people to investigate," Janet said, carrying a tray of cooled scones up front to put them in the display case. Debbie followed her with another tray. "Though I guess we don't know it was about destroying police evidence for sure, since other departments also use that warehouse."

"Yeah, but it seems the most likely scenario, doesn't it?" Debbie asked.

Janet nodded. "Anyway, there's no one better to investigate this than Ian and his team. And in the meantime, we're going to have a busy few days."

"I sure hope so." Debbie poured herself some coffee from the pot Janet had started earlier. "Kim says they're expecting several hundred people for the homecoming festival and, judging by yesterday, we'll have plenty of customers."

"And our first customer of the day is here." Janet smiled as Patricia Franklin's face appeared in the panel of the glass door. "Good morning," she called out as Patricia stepped inside the café. Debbie was already steaming the milk for the peppermint mocha that their friend ordered every day.

"Hey. It's a hot one, isn't it?" Patricia smiled as she approached the counter. She wore a crisp white sleeveless blouse and carried a navy blue blazer over her arm.

"It's summer in Ohio," Janet said with a grimace. "You know, we could make your mocha iced." She didn't understand how Patricia could drink the Christmassy drink in July—and drink it hot at that.

"No thanks," Patricia replied. "I'm a creature of habit, I'm afraid. And I've got a big day, so I need all the caffeine I can get. I can't have all that ice watering down my drink."

"Are you working a big case?" Debbie asked, pouring the milk into a to-go cup. Patricia was a private-practice lawyer, and she often worked on a number of cases at once.

"Not so much a big one as a big day for an important one," Patricia said.

Janet wanted to ask what she meant, but she knew from experience that Patricia wouldn't say. She took her clients' privacy very seriously, which was only one of the reasons she had such an excellent reputation.

"Well, I hope it goes well." Debbie added the mint syrup, espresso, and chocolate to the milk in Patricia's cup and topped it with whipped cream before putting on the lid.

"And I hope this gives you the strength you need on this momentous day," Janet said. "If you need more, we're here."

Patricia laughed. "I'll keep that in mind."

After Patricia left, several of their other regulars walked in. Ashling Kelly ordered an iced coffee, and Mark Thomas, the handyman at the museum who had been at the warehouse fire, ordered a black drip and a chocolate chip muffin. Harry Franklin—Patricia's grandfather and former porter and conductor at the Dennison station—came in like he always did with Crosby, his faithful canine companion, beside him.

"How are you today, Harry?" Janet asked.

"The Lord woke me up this morning, so I'm not complaining," Harry replied. He took a seat, and Crosby took his usual place at his feet.

"That's a good attitude."

She offered him a laminated menu, but he waved it away. "Eggs and toast, please," he said.

"And some for Crosby as well." Janet put the menu back. "Coming right up."

Harry, like his granddaughter, was a creature of habit. He came by the café for breakfast most days, and after he finished, he often sat on a bench on the platform to watch the trains go by. Passenger trains didn't stop at the depot anymore except for the Christmas trains that ran during the holidays, but the long-haul trains still used the tracks, and Harry liked to see them go rushing past.

It was a busy morning, and even though Wednesdays weren't typically their biggest days, they were kept hopping with all the extra people in town for the festival. On one of her trips into the dining room Janet chatted with a representative from a local bank chain who was in town to help veterans get low-interest housing loans. Another time she exchanged ideas with the woman who was in charge of running the lighting and electrical for the outdoor film to be shown on a big screen Friday night. But mostly she worked in the kitchen, filling orders as quickly as she could.

She was carrying another tray of scones to the display case when she saw that the antique-firearms dealer who had been in the café the day before was back. Janet took the receipt she'd found from her pocket, along with a menu, and approached his table. "It's good to see you again," she said, handing him the menu. "How are you enjoying your time in Dennison?"

"It's been eventful," he said. He had a mane of gray hair and a mustache. There was a bandage on his wrist, and he had grazes on one cheek. Had those been there yesterday? Janet couldn't remember.

"In a good way, I hope."

"Let's just say this café is the bright spot," he said. "I'll have another one of those turkey clubs with fries."

"Coming right up." Janet took the menu back. "After you left yesterday, I found this under your table. Is it yours, by any chance?"

She held out the receipt, and he peered at it. Then his eyes widened, and he snatched it from her hand. "You found that here?"

"I guess it must have fallen out of your bag." Was she imagining it, or did he seem panicked? "I wasn't sure if it was yours, but I saved it in case it was important."

"It's—" He shoved the receipt into his pants pocket. "I don't know how that—" He peeked under the table, as if the answer might be there. "Anyway, that turkey club?"

"Sure thing. I'll get that right out to you."

He didn't respond but pulled out his phone and started typing on it.

Janet tried not to think too much of it as she walked away. It had been an odd exchange, but she didn't know him, nor did she know what was going on in his life. Besides, she had plenty of work to keep her busy. She went back into the kitchen, checked the orders, and started making burgers and sandwiches. She was glad Paulette was there to help. Her sweet demeanor and wide smile always made customers happy.

As the rush died down, Janet left the kitchen and noticed a small crowd gathering outside the museum. Kim Smith stood near the newest Pullman car that had been meticulously restored and transformed into a bed and breakfast over the past year. The first Pullman had opened for overnight guests last year, and Kim had been working on getting this one restored and up and running for quite some time. Janet had seen the workers—plumbers, electricians, upholsterers, historic-preservation specialists—come and go for so long that it was hard to believe the work was finally done.

Kim stood beside Jim Watson from the newspaper. Marty Blair, from the mayor's office, was also there. Kim had mentioned that she'd called the newspaper about the official opening of the second Pullman, and Janet realized she must be giving them a tour.

"I can't imagine sleeping in a train car by choice," Paulette said. "Not when there are perfectly good motels out by the highway. I think I'd get claustrophobic."

"I think it sounds kind of neat," Debbie said. "It would be like the glory days of train travel, but you don't have to go anywhere."

"And your table and bench turn into a bed. That part is cool," Janet added.

"Give me a king-size mattress and a hotel pool any day," Paulette said with a laugh. "But I do hope it goes well for Kim. She's worked so hard to make this happen."

"I hope so too," Janet agreed. The renovation had taken longer and cost more than Kim had anticipated, as so many renovations did.

She was glad for Kim that it was finally opening and the museum would begin to see a return on its investment.

After the lunch rush, the café emptied out, and they started to clean up in preparation for closing. Janet was wiping off the tables while Paulette swept, and Debbie was closing out the register when the door opened and a tall African American man walked in. He appeared to be in his sixties or seventies, and he wore a hat that said ARMY VETERAN. Janet guessed he'd served in Vietnam.

"I'm afraid we're closing for the day," she told him. "But we'll be open again at seven tomorrow morning."

"That's okay," he said. "I was actually wondering if you might be able to help me find Harry Franklin. Do you know him?" The man was soft-spoken, with bronze skin, warm brown eyes, and white hair.

"Sure." Janet straightened. "We know Harry. He's here nearly every day."

"I was hoping to speak with him. I used to know where his family lived, but it seems they've moved since I saw him last."

"I'm not sure where he is at the moment," Janet said. "I could give him a call, if you'd like." She didn't feel comfortable giving the man Harry's address.

"I would appreciate that," he said.

Janet took her cell phone from her apron pocket and tried Harry's number. It rang and rang, and then it went to voice mail.

"I'm sorry, but he didn't pick up," she said. "If you come back in the morning, I bet you'll be able to catch him. He comes by here most days, and then he often goes out to the tracks to watch the trains go by."

The man nodded. "Thank you for your help. I'll try to catch him in the morning."

"What's your name?" Debbie asked. "If we see him, we'll tell him to watch for you."

"John," he said, and then he left.

When the door had closed behind him, Janet turned to Debbie. "Long-lost friend?"

Debbie shrugged. "No idea. But we'll see if he finds Harry tomorrow, I guess."

They finished cleaning up the café, and Janet closed out the cash register and sorted through the day's receipts. She was about to set them aside when one in particular caught her eye.

CHAPTER FOUR

*J*anet looked down at the credit card receipt in her hand. *Jedidiah Merrick* was scrawled across the bottom. She'd seen the name Merrick this morning. It had been on Ian's list of potential suspects. People who had items in the police evidence section of the warehouse. He had been in here today.

She went over the items listed on the receipt. A turkey club, paid for at 11:34 at table 7. That was the antique-firearms dealer who had dropped the receipt from the army surplus store. *He* was Jedidiah Merrick? The one Ian had listed as a suspect in the warehouse fire?

Janet thought back over the brief exchange they'd had. He'd said his time in Dennison had been "eventful." He had grazes on his cheek and a bandage on his wrist, and she wasn't sure he'd had them yesterday. And when she'd given him his receipt, the one from the army surplus store, he'd acted strangely. Why? She tried to remember what had been on the receipt. Some kind of glass bottle, rope, gloves, and a knife.

"Oh my." She put her hand down on the counter to steady herself.

"Everything all right?" Paulette returned the broom to the closet and hung up her apron.

"It's…" Janet struggled to put her thoughts into words. If you filled a glass bottle with a flammable liquid, put rope in it, and lit the rope on fire, you would have an easy way to start a fire. You could toss it and run. "I'm okay. But I think I need to talk to Ian."

She pulled out her phone and called him, but it went straight to voice mail. She used her locator app. As she suspected, he was at the warehouse. She didn't know how long he'd slept, but she wasn't at all surprised to see that he was back at work and looking into the fire.

Maybe she would swing by with some goodies for the officers who were working out there. She was willing to bet Ian hadn't had lunch yet. She could take him a sandwich and some cookies for the other officers on duty. It couldn't hurt. No one was ever sad when someone showed up with treats. And she could tell him about what Jedidiah Merrick had bought at the army surplus store.

She quickly made a ham and cheese sandwich and packed a bunch of cookies and muffins into a paper bag. She told Debbie her plan, as well as her theory about Jedidiah Merrick.

"I thought the antique-gun guy was in town for the festival though," Debbie said. "How could he have anything in the police evidence warehouse?"

"I don't know," Janet said. "He said his time here had been 'eventful.' Maybe he managed to get in trouble with the law already?"

"You think he's the kind of guy who gets arrested on his first night in town?" Debbie frowned. "I thought he seemed nice."

"Ian's note said the evidence in the warehouse connected with him was a Springfield Trapdoor 1873. Is that some kind of gun?"

Debbie pulled out her phone and tapped on it a few times. "Yep. An antique rifle."

"So whatever happened with him, it must have involved one of his antiques. Maybe someone tried to steal it or something."

"Do you think his guns still work?"

"I hope not." Janet folded her arms over her chest. "But we would have heard if someone had been shot, especially if it was with an antique rifle. That would have made the news."

"Well, whatever it was, let's go tell Ian about him."

"You're coming with me?"

"Of course I am."

As they walked to Janet's car, Kim came out of the museum and toward the parking lot. The visitors were gone, and she waved when she saw Janet and Debbie then hurried to join them.

"How did the interview go?" Debbie asked.

"It went really well," Kim said. "Jim took a lot of photos, so hopefully the article will drum up some attention."

"And reservations," Janet added. "I'm sure it will. After all that work, the train car must have turned out beautifully."

"It did. I have to run to a doctor's appointment, but I have a couple of minutes. Would you like to duck in and see it?" Kim asked.

"Can we?" Debbie asked eagerly.

"Sure." Kim beckoned for them to follow her.

She led them across a set of tracks and toward the red train car with the word PENNSYLVANIA written in gold on the side. They walked up a short set of metal steps and entered at the end of a long hallway. The floor was covered in a rich red and gold carpet, and the walls were painted a yellowish gold. Windows lined one side of the hallway, and compartments branched off of it.

"This car is originally from the 1920s, and everything here has been restored to its original state, from the hardware to the fixtures to the carpeting," Kim said as she led them into the first compartment.

It was much like the other Pullman in that there was a table with benches upholstered in pink to its left and right, as well as another pink bench opposite it. "We had some challenges with the craftsmanship in a few places, but we did our best to get the details right."

"I don't see any craftsmanship issues," Debbie said. "It's lovely."

"That table turns into a bed, right?" Janet asked.

"Right," Kim confirmed. "Like in a motor home."

"This one is my favorite," Debbie said, gesturing toward the rounded cabinet near the ceiling.

"Mine too." Kim reached above the table and hooked her finger into the round slot in the cabinet. When she pulled down, a sleeping berth emerged. "By the time you were ready for bed at night, the porter would have already come through and set everything up for you."

Janet pointed to the ladder that led to the berth. "I would probably fall off that thing."

"It's sturdier than it looks," Kim assured her.

Janet saw a small sink in the corner of the compartment, and windows lined one wall, above the table, like in the other Pullman car.

"There's a bathroom in here." Kim opened a wooden door and showed them the compact space. "We did these a little differently, with newer fixtures, even though they have the same old-fashioned style. And there's a full bathroom with a shower that guests can use at the far end, in the hospitality suite."

Janet had seen that in the other car. Kim kept the suite stocked with coffee, snacks, bottles of water, and games.

"Can you imagine traveling like this?" Janet ran her hand over the soft upholstery. "On my last flight, my knees were in my ears."

"It really was another time," Kim said. "Of course, you could be on the train for days at a time instead of just hours, so there is that."

"I wouldn't mind being on a train for days with a setup like this," Debbie said. "It's so cool that you've restored it to its former glory."

"Well, don't examine it too closely." Kim grimaced. "Not all of it could stand up to close scrutiny. I'm just glad it's finally done. It's been a long road."

"But it was worth it." Debbie smiled. "I'm sure you'll have people lining up to rent it out."

"Let's hope so." Kim led them from the train car, and they walked to the parking lot together then parted ways to go to their cars.

Janet set the goodies in the back seat and climbed into the driver's seat.

"Did Kim seem a little off to you when she showed us the Pullman?" Debbie asked as they pulled out of the parking lot. She cranked up the air and adjusted the vent so that it faced her.

"She was definitely concerned about the quality of some of the work," Janet said. "Which I didn't understand. It looked great to me." As she drove down the street, something nagged at the back of her mind. Something about the contractor. Something about upholstery. Something about—

"Todd Mills," she blurted.

Debbie stared at her as if she were crazy. "What about Todd Mills?"

"Todd Mills is the contractor who restored the Pullman, isn't he?" She and Debbie had met him several times. He'd restored the first Pullman, and Kim had hired him again when it was time to renovate the second one. Todd was a historic-preservation specialist who had worked on some impressive projects all over the state. He lived locally, and Kim was lucky that he'd been able to fit the Pullman renovations into his schedule, as he was often booked out for months.

"You know he was. Why do you ask?"

"There was a Mills on Ian's list of people who had evidence in the police warehouse."

"And you think it's Todd Mills?"

"Ian wrote 'upholstery' beside his name, so I'm guessing it's him."

"Why would there be evidence against Todd Mills in the warehouse?"

"I don't know," Janet said. "But it seems possible that it might have something to do with the Pullman."

"Kim is on her way to the doctor, or else I'd say we should go back and ask her about him," Debbie said. "How about I call her?"

"That's a good idea. She might not tell us anything, but it can't hurt to ask."

Debbie tried Kim but must not have gotten an answer, so she left a message. "Hi, Kim, it's Debbie. Thanks so much for the tour of the new Pullman. Janet and I thought of a question about the contractor you used, so would you call me back when you get a chance? Hope your doctor's appointment goes well."

Debbie put her phone down and said to Janet, "I'll let you know if she answers. So, what are we searching for at the scene of the fire?"

"Nothing, really. We're going to tell Ian about what the antique-firearms dealer bought at the army surplus store."

"Right. But what are we looking for at the scene?"

"We're not looking for anything."

"Uh-huh." Debbie raised an eyebrow at her. "If you say so."

When they pulled up in front of the warehouse a few minutes later, Janet saw several police cars, and the whole area was marked off with yellow caution tape. Areas within the taped-off section were surrounded by more tape or circled with spray-on chalk. Evidence to be logged, most likely. What used to be the warehouse was now a shell of twisted blackened metal. The whole thing hadn't burned down. There were sections that still stood. But she suspected the smoke would have damaged most if not all of whatever was inside. The whole place smelled like the inside of a chimney.

"Oh my," Debbie said as they stepped out of the car. The July heat hung like a blanket over the scene. Officers were bent over one of the chalk circles with their heads together, in low conversation, but they all looked up when Janet's car door closed. Ian's gaze found them.

"We brought goodies." Janet held up the bag of treats. "To help fuel your investigation."

Deputy Brendan Vaughn's face brightened, and the new officer, Ethan Meyers, stepped toward them. Captain Hernandez, who had been conversing with Ian over the chalk circle inside the caution tape, smiled at them. Only Ian seemed skeptical.

"This is an active crime scene," Ian said, pointing at the caution tape that surrounded the area. His face glistened with sweat. She didn't know how they could stand wearing those long-sleeved uniform shirts in the unrelenting heat. "I'm afraid you can't be here."

"We won't stick around," Janet said. "But I guessed you hadn't had lunch, so I brought you a sandwich. And there are cookies and muffins for the rest of the squad."

Ian walked over to her, staying on the other side of the caution tape, and took the paper bag. "Thank you," he said. "That was thoughtful. I am hungry."

"I figured you would be." She smiled. "You couldn't have gotten much sleep, and I knew you wouldn't stop to eat."

"I appreciate it," he said, pulling out the sandwich she'd wrapped in butcher paper.

"There are all kinds of cookies and muffins too."

"I'll take those." Brendan walked over and took the bag out of Ian's hands. He gave her a smile that Janet knew had charmed several of the single women in town. "Snack time!" he called out.

Ethan hurried to Brendan's side, peered into the bag, and retrieved a chocolate chip cookie.

"Also, I wanted to tell you about something that happened at the café that I think might be relevant," Janet said to Ian.

"What's that?"

"We had a customer come in yesterday for lunch. An antique-firearms dealer by the name of Jedidiah Merrick."

That got his attention. Ian narrowed his eyes.

"He dropped a receipt yesterday, from the army surplus store in New Philadelphia. I saved it in case he needed it. He came back in today, so I gave it to him. And he acted a little strange when I gave it to him."

"How so?"

"He grabbed it and shoved it into his pocket. And then he wouldn't make eye contact with me. He also had scratches on his face and a bandage on his wrist, though I don't remember if he had them yesterday."

"Do you remember what was on the receipt?" Ian asked.

"It was for a glass bottle, some rope, and gloves," Janet said. "And some T-shirts. Maybe something else? A knife, I think."

"Did you take a picture of the receipt before giving it to him?"

"No. I didn't think it was anything important. It was only afterward that I realized those things could have been used, along with some kind of flammable liquid, to make something that would start a fire. So I thought you should know."

Janet hadn't mentioned seeing Merrick's name in Ian's notebook, but that didn't seem to matter. Ian nodded, and Captain Hernandez, next to him, wrote something on a small pad.

"Thank you for letting us know," Ian said. "That's good information."

"I'm glad to help. Let me know if there's anything else I can do."

"Are you finding much of anything?" Debbie asked. "I imagine a fire doesn't leave many clues behind."

"There are actually more than you'd think," Ian said, gesturing around at the circles that contained evidence. "The state inspector was here earlier, and he was able to tell a lot about how the fire started and spread. The fire itself didn't erase the clues. It's all the spectators who showed up last night and possibly trampled over the evidence that would let us follow the arsonist's trail." He nodded at Janet. "Present company excepted."

Janet laughed. "I didn't exactly come in search of a good time."

"What kind of evidence have you found so far?" Debbie asked. "Anything that points to who did this?"

"I'm afraid I can't tell you that, no matter how grateful I am for this." Ian held up his sandwich. "But thank you for bringing it by."

Janet knew she was being dismissed, and as much as she wanted to stay, she had to leave them to their task. "You're welcome."

The officers chorused their thanks and moved away to get back to work.

Janet started toward the car again but froze when Debbie said, "A Black Jack gum wrapper."

"What?"

Debbie pointed at a scrap of paper in the center of a chalk circle on the other side of the crime-scene tape. "It's a Black Jack gum wrapper."

Debbie was right. Janet recognized the distinctive blue-and-black wrapper. Why was a Black Jack gum wrapper being catalogued as evidence at the scene of the fire?

CHAPTER FIVE

"How many packs of Black Jack have we sold recently?" Debbie asked when they were back in Janet's car.

"Maybe a couple," Janet said. "Not too many. But other places sell it."

"Not in Dennison," Debbie said. "At least, not that I'm aware of. It's just us and the museum. That particular brand isn't easy to come by. There can't be that much of a demand for it. I would think people buy it mostly for nostalgic reasons."

"Right. It does have a unique flavor. You either love it or you hate it," Janet said.

"Licorice-flavored gum is not my idea of a good time, but some people must like it, since they're still making it," Debbie said.

"It's definitely one-of-a-kind."

"The fact that we're one of two places in town who sell it, and we don't sell very much of it, means we can probably talk to Kim and narrow down who could have dropped it pretty easily."

But Janet didn't need to think too much to narrow it down. She already had a suspect in mind. "Tyler Wilson."

"His parents bought some Black Jack gum at the café yesterday, didn't they?"

"They bought it for Tyler," Janet said. "And Wilson was one of the names in Ian's list. There must have been some kind of evidence against Tyler in the warehouse."

"Though, to be fair, Ian did say there were a lot of spectators at the fire," Debbie said. "Any of them could have dropped the gum wrapper."

"I suppose that's true," Janet said. "It wouldn't have had to be the perpetrator. Who else have we sold Black Jack gum to recently?"

"On Saturday a couple on a road trip from New York to San Francisco bought some," Debbie said. "They were stopping at interesting attractions and historical sites along the way. But surely they're several states away by now."

"They don't seem likely," Janet said. "I've sold a few packs here and there but mostly to tourists, like those road-trippers. Not to people in town."

"Do you think we should go back and tell Ian?" Debbie asked.

Janet thought about it for a moment. Ian didn't want them at the scene of the fire. "Nah. I'll tell him when he gets home tonight."

"Okay," Debbie said. "Did you hear what Brendan and that new guy—Meyers, I think—were talking about when we walked up?"

"I didn't. What was it?"

"They said something about the building's security system. So I looked around, and there was a security camera over the door, but it was broken."

"You mean it was destroyed by the fire?"

"Not that I could tell, but I'm not sure how they'd figure that out. The glass was cracked for sure, though I don't know if that happened during the fire or before it or what. All I know is that the officers were very interested in whatever happened to that security camera."

"And no doubt whatever is shown on its footage," Janet added.

"I imagine so," Debbie said. "I'm sure they're already working on getting it."

"Hopefully, that will make it clear who did this." Janet felt better already. "Between the receipt and the gum wrapper and the security camera, which might very well have caught whoever set the fire, the police should have the arsonist in custody in no time."

"I hope you're right."

When Janet got home, she took Laddie out for a walk and contemplated dinner. It was too hot to use the oven. Maybe they'd grill. She had some hamburger buns in the freezer and ground beef in the fridge. Burgers, then.

She sat down at the table with a pen and notebook. She scribbled the title *Recipes* on the first page. She had asked her old boss, Charla Whipple from the Third Street Bakery, to take over the baking for the café while she was on vacation, and even though that was a week and a half away, it didn't hurt to get a jump on things. She would make a list of recipes for Charla to use while she was gone. Janet also wanted to bake and freeze some muffins and scones and such to supplement the daily baking, but Charla would still have plenty to make each day. She made a list of the café's bestsellers—blueberry muffins, peaches-and-cream scones, cinnamon rolls, chocolate chip cookies—and started gathering the recipes. They were all simple enough to make, and everyone loved them.

Then she flipped to another page in her notebook and wrote *Packing List*. She started to write down all the things they would need to take to the lake.

Clothes for hot and cool weather, since the temperature could swing widely out there.

Chargers and cords for their electronics.

Bathing suits and beach towels. Sunscreen for sure. Did they have sunscreen? She remembered that Tiffany had taken the bottle from the bathroom to the pool and kept it in her locker there. They would need more. So Janet moved to another page in her notebook and wrote *Shopping List* at the top.

Sunscreen.

Bug spray, and plenty of it.

A new cooler. Theirs had given up the ghost after a church picnic last summer.

Food—but then, they would buy what they needed for the week at the grocery store near the lake house. So she started a new list on a new page: *To buy at the lake.*

Bread, milk, coffee, cereal, chicken, pasta…

After twenty minutes, she'd written down everything she could think of and she'd also started two more lists: *Things to ask Ian and/ or Tiffany about* and *Things to ask the cottage owner about.*

There was so much to keep track of to get ready to go on vacation. It would be worth it when they were there, but it required a lot of preparation.

After she'd made her lists, Janet tried to relax with a book, but her mind kept going back to the fire and the evidence they'd found. Tyler and Jedidiah had been on Ian's list. So had Todd Mills. And there was one other person. Ward, whoever that was. That person's items in the warehouse had indicated arson.

Janet turned to a fresh sheet in her notebook and wrote down the information she remembered from Ian's list, so she wouldn't forget.

Ward—gas can? Something about a wall
Tyler Wilson—beer cans, parts of the car
Todd Mills—upholstery? Something electrical. Thumb drive
Jedidiah Merrick—Springfield Trapdoor 1873

She scanned the list, hoping it would tell her something she didn't already know, but nothing jumped out at her. She ripped the page out of the notebook, folded it, tucked it into her book, and tried to focus. Finally, she gave up and started dinner.

Tiffany came home just as Janet was pulling the ground beef from the fridge. She smelled like chlorine and sunscreen, and she wore red shorts and a lifeguard shirt over her swimsuit.

"You're making lists. We must be getting close to vacation." Tiffany bent over the notebook, flipping the pages, then picked up the pen and started writing.

"What are you adding?"

"Potato chips and dip," Tiffany said. "And those ice pops I like. Some other stuff, like new water shoes. Mine are falling apart." She moved to a different list and wrote on it. "And I could use some new shorts too."

"Hey now. This isn't a chance to go on a shopping spree."

"You don't want me to run around with no pants on, do you?" Tiffany teased.

"You used to when you were little."

Janet had so many happy memories from those days, when she and Ian and Tiffany splashed in the lake and lolled on the dock. They'd lived in their swimsuits and flip-flops. Those were simpler times, when Tiffany was content with a bucket and shovel and she and Ian could sit on the porch and read and chat for days on end. All they'd needed was one another. She didn't have to worry about where Tiffany was going or who she was with. Janet thought back to how hard she'd cried after she dropped Tiffany off for her first day of kindergarten. She thought she'd worried a lot then. She'd had no idea how difficult it would be to watch her daughter step out into the world on her own. Tiffany was doing great, but sometimes she missed that little kid.

"There's a lot about those days at the lake that I'd like to recreate," Tiffany said, straightening up. "But that is not one of them. How long until dinner?"

Janet glanced at the clock. "Probably an hour or so, assuming your dad comes home on time."

"Cool. Enough time for me to go on a run." Janet heard her footsteps vanishing toward her room.

Ian came home a little later than usual, and though Janet could see the worry and stress etched on his face, he grilled the burgers while she put together a salad and Tiffany set the table. They ate on the back deck, with the cool evening breeze blowing the heat of the day away and then carried their plates inside. Tiffany grabbed her car keys and headed out to see her friends, leaving Janet and Ian behind to clean up the kitchen.

"How is the investigation going?" she asked as she stacked the leftover burgers into a storage container.

"Frustrating," Ian said, scraping a plate before he set it in the dishwasher. "Usually we're looking for suspects, for anyone with a motive. In this case, we had several cases with evidence stored in the warehouse, which means we have very obvious potential suspects, each with a clear motive."

"That sounds like a good thing to me."

"Well, yes." Ian dumped the dregs of a glass of lemonade into the sink and set the glass in the top rack of the dishwasher. "I suppose it's not the worst problem to have. But the thing is, we have virtually nothing to indicate any of them were involved. Though we're checking out Jedidiah Merrick. That receipt was a good find."

"He sure acted funny when I gave it back to him."

"And the list of things he bought is mighty suspicious. That was well-spotted."

"Thank you." Janet snapped the lid on the container. "Debbie noticed something else when we were at the scene of the fire this afternoon."

"Oh yeah?"

"There was a gum wrapper in a chalk circle near where we were standing."

"Yes, we found that."

"Well, it was Black Jack gum. It's a nostalgic brand we sell at the café. Debbie and I are pretty sure we're the only place in town that sells it, along with the museum." She slid the container into a free spot in the refrigerator.

Ian must have already known that, but he didn't indicate one way or the other. "Do you remember who has recently bought this particular brand of gum from you?"

"I can make a list for you, and I'm sure Kim could make one of the people who bought it at the museum. But one name came to mind immediately. Carrie and Austin Wilson were at the café yesterday, and they bought a pack of Black Jack gum and said it was for Tyler."

"Really?" Ian raised an eyebrow.

"Really. And—" She paused for a moment. She might as well confess. "This morning I saw that your notebook was open to a list of names. It wasn't hard to guess that it was of the people who had police evidence in the warehouse and what the evidence was."

Ian sighed. "I saw it like that when I came downstairs this morning. I need to be more careful." He put another plate into the dishwasher. "Is that how you knew to bring us info about that receipt?"

Janet nodded. "I mean, once I realized what the items on the receipt could be used for, I knew it was worth telling you anyway. But yes, when I saw the name Jedidiah Merrick on a credit card receipt from the café, I remembered it from the list and knew I needed to tell you."

"I'm glad you did," Ian said. "And the tip about the gum wrapper is a good one too."

Janet slipped the leftover buns into their bag and slid it into the bread drawer. "Did any of the evidence in the warehouse survive the fire?"

"Some," Ian said. "I can't tell you much, but here's what I can tell you. The fire was started on purpose. The fire investigator confirmed that today. He says the burn pattern makes a clear case for arson. He can tell by the way it burned that there was an accelerant used."

"Like gasoline?"

"Exactly like gasoline."

"It's amazing he can tell all that from a burned-out warehouse." It had been nothing more than a blackened shell to Janet.

"A lot of people think fire is a good way to cover up crimes, assuming it will burn everything away, but fire leaves clues behind like anything else."

"What about the other departments that had things stored in the warehouse?" Janet asked. "Is there any chance someone set the fire because of something they had rather than the police evidence?"

"We're exploring that possibility, of course. There have been a few theories floated from other departments in town. The parks department told us about a lifeguard they recently fired because he wouldn't stay off his phone on the lifeguard stand. Apparently, he blew up and told his manager and everyone who was around they'd be sorry. Maybe this was his revenge."

"That's interesting," Janet said.

Ian shrugged. "Or maybe it was someone who didn't like the town's Christmas decorations, or had it out for the Fourth of July dunk tank. And the fire department told us about a prospective volunteer firefighter who got mad and threatened the fire chief when he didn't pass the training. Or it could have been someone from the mayor's office, or the depot museum, or any other group that stores items in that warehouse. We're checking into every possibility we can think of."

"The museum has stuff stored there?"

"Sure. Old displays, items they haven't catalogued, and things like that. But the fact is, the police evidence was in its own part of the warehouse, in a locked cage, and that's where the investigator says the fire started. It seems too intentional not to assume our primary suspects were interested in getting rid of evidence in that particular section of the warehouse."

They worked in silence while Janet mulled over everything. She realized she had one big question based on what Ian had told her.

"How did he get in?" she finally asked. "The person who set the fire, I mean. If the police section of the warehouse was under lock and key."

"That's what doesn't make sense about any of this."

"What?"

"There was no sign of forced entry," Ian said, shaking his head. "The warehouse had a steel door, so aside from some soot, it remained pretty much intact. You can see clear as day that the door wasn't forced open. The lock wasn't damaged. Neither was the lock on the cage that holds all the police evidence."

"If the warehouse is used by different departments in town, don't lots of people have keys?"

"Yes, many people have keys to the warehouse, but there are only two keys to the evidence cage. I have one of them, and the other is kept at the station. Whoever started the fire started it inside the cage, so someone must have gotten in there somehow."

Janet thought about this. "What's the cage made of?"

"Chain-link fencing," Ian said.

"They couldn't have sprayed gasoline into the cage and tossed in a match from outside the fence?"

"The fire inspector doesn't think so. He thinks someone was physically inside the evidence cage."

"Which makes it pretty clear that someone specifically wanted to get rid of police evidence."

"That's the conclusion I came to as well," Ian said. "The fact that it started in the evidence cage is a detail no one knows except a few officers at the station, the fire inspector, and now you. Please don't let that get out."

"Of course," Janet said. "None of this can get out. I won't repeat anything."

"Thank you."

"So how did the arsonist get into the cage?" Janet asked.

"We don't know."

There had to be an explanation. "Who had access to the key? Not yours. The other one."

"Just guys on the police force."

"Do you think one of them did it?"

"No," he said, a little forcefully. "No way."

But something in his face made her think he wasn't so sure.

CHAPTER SIX

John took a handkerchief out of his pocket and wiped his brow. The summer sun was hot, and he'd had to walk here from the bus stop. Only a mile, but it felt like more in this heat.

He put the handkerchief back in his pocket then checked the address and read the words over the door. NEW PHILADELPHIA ARMY RECRUITING STATION. This was it. This was his chance.

"Good afternoon." The man behind the counter gave him a once-over. "What brings you here today?"

"I'm here to join up."

"How old are you?"

"Eighteen last week, sir."

"Do you have some ID?"

"Yes, sir." He pulled his wallet out of his pocket and slid his ID across the counter.

"What make you want to join the army"—the man glanced at his ID card—"John?"

"I want to serve my country." It was the answer he'd prepared in advance, the one he thought would make the army happiest. He couldn't very well tell them the truth—that he had to get out of this town, this life, and this was the only option he had.

"You know there's a war on, don't you?" The man cocked his head.

"I do, sir. I want to serve my country." College wasn't an option. They could never afford that, though his teachers said he was smart enough. Daddy wanted him to come work at the factory, but John couldn't do it. He wouldn't do it. There was more to life than staying in the same town, doing the same hard job for not enough money. John wanted better. He would do better. If the army was his chance to get out of here, he would take it.

"A lot of people are saying they don't like that we're over there in Vietnam," the recruiter said. "That we shouldn't be there. What do you think?"

Better to get shot at in the jungles of Vietnam than stay here and die a slow death from suffocation. He didn't see how so many people could settle for living like that. Not him. He would get out and make *something of himself. He would be rich someday, or he would die trying.*

"I want to serve my country." As he said it a third time, the man's face broke into a smile.

"In that case, come on back," he said, gesturing to an open area behind the counter. "We'll get you started on your paperwork right away."

Janet couldn't get her mind to settle. She tossed and turned until she finally gave up around one o'clock and climbed out of bed. Sometimes a snack and a book helped settle her mind enough so she could sleep.

Ian didn't stir as she left the room. She crept downstairs and poured a bowl of cornflakes, sat at the kitchen table, and opened her book. The list she'd made earlier fell out.

Ward—gas can? Something about a wall
Tyler Wilson—beer cans, parts of the car
Mills—upholstery? Something electrical. Thumb drive
Merrick—Springfield Trapdoor 1873

Janet knew she should focus on reading and shutting her mind off, but all she wanted to do was find out more about the names on this list. She got up and grabbed her laptop. This was probably the worst thing she could do—blue light from the computer screen was more likely to wake her brain up even more—but she had a suspicion that answers were the one thing that would actually help.

Janet opened up a browser window and tried to figure out what to type. She wanted to know about this Ward person. Someone who had previously committed arson seemed like a good place to start. She typed in the words *Ward fire Dennison*, and the first thing that came up was an article from a month ago in the *Gazette*.

No Injuries Reported at House Fire

The fire department responded to a call of a fire at 548 Clasp Hollow Road and battled the flames for nearly an hour before they were extinguished. The fire was reported by a neighbor, who saw and smelled the smoke. The Dennison fire department—mostly made up of volunteers—arrived quickly and fought the flames using the force's pumper truck as well as water from a nearby creek.

The building had been unoccupied for more than five years, since the owner, Florence Ward, had been moved to a nursing home, reported Fred Wingerson, a neighbor.

"The house had fallen into really bad disrepair," Wingerson told the Gazette. *"Part of the roof had caved in, and the place was crawling with rodents. We called the city to report the dangerous conditions several times over the years, but no one ever did anything. And now look what's happened."*

Firefighters reported that no one was inside the building at the time of the fire and there were no injuries. Asked about the cause of the blaze, Fire Chief Mike Gleason said, "We are still investigating and will not speculate."

The house was owned by Florence Ward, but she had lived in a nursing home for five years before the house burned. She couldn't be the Ward that was on Ian's list.

Janet scrolled down the page and saw several comments.

That place has been an eyesore for years. Glad someone finally did something about it.

Will not speculate? That means they know what happened and are just trying to find proof.

Praise God no one was hurt!

No doubt faulty electrical. It often happens with buildings left to fall apart like this one. Maybe one of those rodents chewed through a wire.

This was arson, clear as day. How do the police not see this?

I live out that way and saw a car speeding away from the area Friday night. I contacted the police to report it, but no one has called me back.

Wonder if they've considered spontaneous combustion? Or aliens?

And that was why they always said not to read the comments.

Janet clicked out of the article and searched for more on the fire. She found a short follow-up piece in the police blotter section of the newspaper. It reported that Jennie Ward had been arrested in connection with a suspicious fire of a derelict building on Clasp Hollow Road on June 24. There wasn't much information in the short entry, but it gave Janet the information she needed. Jennie Ward.

She opened a new browser window and typed in *Jennie Ward*. She found several social media profiles, including one that she guessed was the right Jennie. She lived in Dennison, Ohio, and looked to be in her midforties, with short brownish-blond hair and brown eyes. The page mostly featured photos of Jennie hunting and fishing with a bald man by her side. The page hadn't been active in over a year. This was probably her, but it didn't tell Janet very much and gave no information about the fire. Where could she find out more about that?

She navigated to the Tuscarawas County website and made her way to the page for the clerk of the courts. Court records were public. A few minutes later, she was reading the court stenographer's transcription of Jennie Ward's arraignment.

Jennie was charged with arson and had pleaded not guilty. From comments made by the judge, it became clear that the house had belonged to Jennie's mother, Florence Ward, and had been left empty when Florence was moved to a nursing home. Florence had recently died, and the house had passed to her only child, Jennie.

The judge had asked Jennie why the house hadn't been cared for or sold since Florence had moved out, and Jennie said she couldn't afford the maintenance that such a large house required on top of her own home. The judge also asked about an insurance policy that had been taken out on the house earlier in the year, shortly after Florence had passed away. Jennie told him that once the house had officially passed to her, she'd wanted to protect it.

Based on the judge's comments, it was clear he hadn't believed her story, and he'd asked about the rather convenient timing of the fire—mere weeks after the insurance policy had been taken out—but Jennie denied that she had anything to do with the fire. The transcript ended abruptly at the bottom of the last page.

What a sad tale.

There was no record in the transcript of the evidence the fire and police departments had against Jennie that had led to her being charged with the crime—that would come out at the trial—but the police must have possessed evidence against her. And Janet knew that the evidence included a gas can and something about a piece of the wall. That was what had been in the police evidence section of the warehouse. But now that the evidence had been destroyed, would Jennie be held accountable?

She dug around online for a while longer, hoping to find out more about the fire on Clasp Hollow Road but found nothing useful.

Janet finished her bowl of cereal but still wasn't sleepy, so she decided to try to find out more about Tyler Wilson's accident. She felt bad for him. He'd had it tough. He'd been a big baseball star at the local high school and had been recruited to play in college. Anyone would have thought he'd been elected to the White House, given how proud Carrie Wilson had been. It must have been so hard to have an injury take all that away.

Janet went back to the newspaper archive and found a short article about the accident. The single-car crash had occurred at 12:17 a.m. on May 18 on Skyview Road. That was a rural road outside of town. The police had responded when a neighbor heard the screech of tires and then a crash as the car skidded off the road and hit a tree. Tyler was found walking down the road away from the abandoned vehicle. He had been treated for minor injuries. Tyler failed field sobriety tests, and empty beer cans were found in his car, but Tyler had refused a breath test. The article noted that failure to submit to the test resulted in an automatic one-year driver's license suspension.

The article was accompanied by photos that showed the front of the car crumpled against a tree. Broken glass glinted in the black-and-white picture. Janet shuddered. It was a wonder Tyler hadn't been killed. But the fact that he'd left the scene and refused a breath test didn't look great for him. The court records showed he'd been arraigned on May twenty-fifth and had pled not guilty, which was no doubt why whatever evidence the police had against him was stored in the warehouse, awaiting the trial.

What about Jedidiah Merrick? Janet typed his name into the browser and found his website, which showcased antique firearms he had for sale. Janet didn't know much about guns, especially antiques, so she clicked through his site quickly and realized there wasn't much useful there. The address given for the business was a post office box in Grove City, Ohio, a suburb of Columbus.

She did a new search for *Jedidiah Merrick Columbus* and found an article in the *Columbus Dispatch*. VETERAN STARTS SUCCESSFUL ANTIQUE-FIREARMS BUSINESS, the headline read. Janet read the article, which explained that Jedidiah had always been interested in guns and weaponry and had started collecting antiques as a hobby before it blossomed into a business. It was a nice story but not particularly informative. Digging deeper, she found one more article that mentioned Jedidiah, saying that he had been arrested after a fight erupted outside a bar in Columbus. He had pled guilty to the drunk-and-disorderly charge and was released without incident.

That was it. There wasn't much to go on and nothing to indicate what had led to his having an antique firearm in the police warehouse in Dennison.

What about Todd Mills? Debbie would have let her know if Kim had returned her call about Todd. But why was there evidence against him in the warehouse? What was the story there?

She searched for the name *Todd Mills*. The top link was a website for his company, Mills Contracting and Renovation. Testimonials from several happy clients were posted front and center.

> *Todd did an amazing job of bringing our antique house back to life. I'm so glad I found him.*
> *No one else out there can match his skill and knowledge of historic buildings. I'd use him again in a heartbeat.*

There were also pictures of some of his projects. She admired the coffered ceiling of a house in Pittsburgh and the inlaid floors at another home. There was even a page devoted to his own house, a restored Victorian in the Ohio countryside. It dripped with gingerbread trim and had original leaded stained glass, herringbone floors, and intricately carved fireplace mantels. He'd installed period wallpaper and decorated with reproduction furniture. It was gorgeous.

There wasn't anything that told her what she'd been hoping to learn. But at long last, her eyelids drooped, and she was ready to go back to bed. She could still get another couple hours of sleep if she went to bed now. She'd do more research on Todd Mills tomorrow.

Hopefully, things would be clearer in the morning.

CHAPTER SEVEN

*J*anet groaned when the alarm went off Thursday morning. It was too early to get up, she was sure. But no, it really was time to get going. She rolled out of bed and stumbled down the stairs. She ignored the cereal bowl she'd left in the sink, started the coffee brewing, and then went back upstairs to get dressed.

She was surprised to see that the lights were on. "What are you doing up so early?" she asked Ian.

"There's a lot to do." He met her gaze. "You got up last night. Is everything okay?"

"Yes," she said. "I couldn't stop my mind from spinning."

"Is this about the fire?"

"Unfortunately."

"Please don't worry about it," he said. "We'll find who did it."

Janet gave him a smile, but she knew that she probably wasn't going to be able to stop worrying. She decided to voice an idea she'd had as she was finally falling asleep.

"The fire was started with gasoline, right?" she asked as she pulled on her favorite comfy teal shirt.

"That's what the fire inspector thinks," Ian confirmed.

"So whoever did it would have had to fill a container with gas and bring it with them to the warehouse. Have you gone around to the gas stations to ask about people who have bought gas in cans recently?"

Ian smiled and shook his head. "I told you that you didn't have to worry about this."

"I just thought about it and wondered."

"The answer is yes," Ian said as he buckled his belt. "Brendan went around to most of the gas stations in the area yesterday, and he'll cover the rest today. No one remembers seeing anyone with a gas can at their pumps recently. We're gathering security camera footage to confirm that. It'll be tedious to go through it all, but we're going to do it."

Janet was glad they'd already had her idea, but she wished they'd gotten somewhere with it already.

"Don't worry," Ian said again. He stepped forward and kissed her forehead. "We'll find who did this."

Janet believed him. She really did. But Ian was worried and stressed about the fire, which meant she couldn't *not* care. And the fact that the clues pointed to two people who'd been at the café in recent days made it feel even more personal. As she poured her coffee and headed out to the car, she knew she wouldn't be able to stop thinking about it until the arsonist was caught.

Janet was still pondering the list of suspects when Debbie arrived at the café.

"You look tired," Debbie said, putting her purse beside Janet's. "Are you okay?"

"At least I know you're not going to sugarcoat it," Janet said with a laugh. "I had a hard time sleeping." She tipped muffins out of a tin and set them on the rack to cool. Raspberry and white chocolate today.

"What were you worried about?" Debbie asked.

"What makes you think I was worried?"

"I've known you for decades," Debbie said, raising an eyebrow. "You were worried."

"Fine." Janet sighed and set another muffin on the cooling rack. "I couldn't stop trying to make sense of what happened at the warehouse, so I got up and did some research on the top suspects."

"Learn anything?" Debbie tied on her apron.

"There's Jennie Ward. She's been indicted for setting fire to a house she inherited."

"An obvious link then. If she's done it once…"

"Then there's Tyler Wilson," Janet went on. "He was arrested for driving under the influence."

"The baseball player with the vintage gum."

"That's right. He wrapped his car around a tree. He refused a breath test and pled not guilty."

Debbie poured herself a cup of coffee. "That's a serious enough charge that I could see wanting to have the evidence erased."

"I really don't think it was him though."

"Why not?"

"Tyler's a good kid," Janet insisted. "Carrie's so involved in church, and Austin is a veteran."

"That doesn't mean their son couldn't have set the fire. I'm sure they're very good people, and I'm sure Tyler is too. But that doesn't mean he couldn't have made a very bad decision. Or a series of them."

While the logical part of Janet knew Debbie was right, the other part of her—the one that had watched Tyler grow up—didn't want it to be true. "I hate when you're right."

"Sorry. I can't always help it." Debbie grinned. "But what about his parents?"

"His parents?" Janet wasn't following.

"Their son is in trouble with the law. A drunk-driving conviction probably wouldn't land him in prison if it's his first arrest, but it's the kind of thing that could have serious consequences for his future. It might make it harder for a college to take a chance on offering him a scholarship. What if one of his parents decided to help smooth the way for him?"

Janet gaped at her friend. "You think Carrie Wilson, who's in my mom's Bible study, committed arson?"

"Statistically speaking, it would be more likely to be the dad."

That wasn't any easier for Janet to wrap her head around. "He's a former Marine. He's a nurse who works with sick children. He organized a clothing drive for needy veterans."

"None of which excludes him from consideration. We just said good people sometimes still make bad decisions."

"I really don't think he would have done that."

"I'm merely suggesting it as a possibility. We have to consider everything," Debbie said. "What about that antique-gun dealer?"

"I couldn't find a lot on him. He lives outside of Columbus. He's a veteran. He was arrested once for getting into a fight at a bar. But I haven't been able to figure out why he was arrested in Dennison or why one of his antique guns was in police custody."

"So there's more to learn."

"And then there's Todd Mills. Did Kim ever get back to you about him?"

"Not yet."

"We can follow up with her today," Janet said.

"I thought you weren't looking into this." Debbie gave her a wry smile.

"I'm not. Ian has his whole team on it, and he doesn't need me meddling. But Kim is our friend. And she's the one who hinted at problems with her contractor. We're being good friends by following up. You know, giving her a chance to vent."

Debbie started to reply but stopped when she saw Patricia Franklin opening the door.

Janet started frothing the milk, and soon they were busy making coffee, serving pastries, and frying eggs and bacon. Janet didn't stop moving until Harry Franklin came in.

"Good morning, Harry," she said, as she poured him a cup of coffee. "Did your friend find you?"

"My friend?" Harry laughed. "I don't think so."

"Someone came in here asking about you," Janet explained. "We didn't catch his last name."

"He might have been an army veteran," Debbie added. "Maybe he knew you from the depot."

"We didn't know who he was, and we didn't want to give out your information, but we called you."

"You did?" Harry pulled his cell phone out of his pocket. "Yes, I have a missed call from you. What was his name?"

"John," Debbie said.

"John?" Harry echoed. "That's a very common name for people of a certain generation. I've known dozens of Johns."

"I'm sorry. He rushed out before we could get his last name," Janet said.

"It's all right. But now I'm intrigued," Harry said. "Can you describe him?"

The women gave him all the details they could recall about John's appearance.

"He had glasses and white hair, but I think he's younger than you are," Janet finished.

"Most of us have glasses these days too," Harry said. "Well, we'll see if he shows up, I guess. Crosby and I will be right up front where we're most likely to notice him." He walked to the counter and took a seat, Crosby at his feet.

"We'll let you know if we see him," Debbie promised.

The rest of the day was a blur. They closed and quickly moved through the cleaning. Shortly after Paulette left for the day, Debbie approached Janet, who could tell something was up by the expression on her friend's face.

"What are you scheming about?"

"Well, Kim never called me back."

"I'm sure she's crazy busy with the festival starting tomorrow."

"You're probably right. I'm sure it's not personal. But I was thinking that maybe we could swing by the museum and see if she has a minute to tell us about Todd Mills. If she's too busy, we'll move on."

"Okay." That would be all right. But Debbie was still smiling. She had something else in mind. "What is it?"

"Don't you need to take a load of clothes to the Wilsons?"

"I do," Janet said. "Oh. I see." She took in a breath and let it out slowly. "I do need to take a load of clothes over. But we can't ask anything about the fire, if that's what you're thinking. Ian wouldn't want us interfering."

"We'll bring some cookies as well as the clothes." Debbie gestured at the display case.

"Okay," Janet said. "Let's start with the museum."

After they locked up, they walked over to the museum and asked for Kim.

Hugh Furdale, a new volunteer docent, was behind the front desk. Behind him, the museum was busy with people admiring the displays.

"Hello, Hugh," Janet said. "We're hoping to speak with Kim. Do you happen to know where she is?"

"I think she's outside getting things ready for the festival," Hugh said.

They thanked him and headed outside, toward the area where the festival was being set up. They found Kim in front of a plywood stage, draping red, white, and blue bunting along the front edge.

"That looks great," Janet said.

"It's harder than you'd think to get this stuff level." Kim used a staple gun to secure the bunting and then straightened up. She set down the staple gun and brushed her forearm across her face. "How are you guys? I'm sorry I haven't called you back, Debbie."

"That's okay," Debbie said. "We know you've been busy."

"It's been kind of crazy. But I'm glad the festival is almost here. Hopefully, people will enjoy it. But you wanted to know about Todd, right?"

"That's right," Debbie said. "When you showed us the Pullman, we got the sense that you weren't totally pleased with his work."

Kim laughed. "That's one way of putting it. Actually, the depot board is suing him."

"Why?" Janet asked.

"Because he consistently missed deadlines and gave us shoddy work, which means he's delayed the opening by months. He went way over budget with little to show for it, and he keeps demanding more." She picked up another bunch of bunting. "He billed us for another huge final payment, which is way more than the amount stated in our contract, and he's making everything difficult because we've refused to pay it. We hate to resort to such extremes, but we really have no other recourse. We have to be good stewards of the museum's funds."

"I had no idea, Kim. I'm sorry you're dealing with all of that." Janet wasn't sure what else to say.

"At first, we thought he was the answer to our prayers, living so close and having so much experience. He comes across as personable and friendly, and he obviously knows his stuff. But I think he takes on too many projects or something. Like I said, he wasn't great on the first Pullman renovation, but good enough that we hired him again. This time was different. At first he seemed scattered, but then I started to see what was really going on."

"What do you mean?"

"He'd show up hours later than he'd said he was going to. Or not show up at all on a day he'd said he would."

"Well, that's irritating," Janet said.

"I realize now I should have been paying closer attention, but it wasn't until he started asking for more money that I realized something was wrong."

"When was that?"

"It happened several times. We had a schedule laid out for how much things would cost and when each payment would be released. He was supposed to pay for the supplies for each portion of the renovation out of the fees. But he would come back to me saying the price of the upholstery fabric had gone up and he needed more. Or that the electrician discovered a big problem and we couldn't move forward until he'd rewired the whole place, so we had to pay more to keep the work moving. But when I spoke with the electrician later, he told me his work hadn't changed from what he'd originally quoted. He wasn't sure what Todd was talking about."

"That's very strange."

"The excuses kept piling up, but he wouldn't admit he'd been swindling us. Eventually, we had no choice but to file the lawsuit to get back the money he'd taken." Kim put in the last staple and put the staple gun down again. "Patricia did some digging, and it turns out he used our money for other unfinished projects for irate customers. He's in debt up to his eyeballs."

"I'm so sorry," Janet said.

"But the Pullman seems so nice," Debbie said.

"Like I said, you can't look too closely. He did finish the work in the end but only after we filed the lawsuit against him. He had to rip out much of the upholstery and redo it, as well as take out the hollow doors he'd installed. We'd specified solid-wood doors so that they would be soundproof between compartments as well as historically accurate. But he tried to get away with cheaper materials, even though we'd paid for better ones."

"How unprofessional," Debbie said.

"I don't know how he thought we wouldn't find out. And the curtains! The first ones he installed were made with incredibly cheap fabric. He tried to tell me it was more historically accurate than the initial sample he'd shown me, but it was polyester. They didn't use that for everything back then like they do now, so I knew he was lying. The plumbing had to be redone too. It's fine now, but if you really examine it, there are a lot of places where it's clear things had to be redone."

"That sounds like a very stressful situation." Janet hadn't noticed anything suspicious, and of course she'd trusted Kim and the board to handle their own business next door.

"I wish I'd hired Greg to do the work to begin with. I spoke with him about it when we started work on the second Pullman. Todd had missed enough deadlines on the first one that I was nervous about hiring him again. It was nothing like what happened this time around, or obviously I wouldn't have. But Greg said he didn't have the expertise to get all the historic details right. That was one thing Todd claimed expertise in, so we went with him against my better judgment. I so wish I'd heeded those red flags. I think Greg would have done a better job in the end, and he's a lot less shady."

"He's not shady at all," Debbie said with a proud smile.

"And then there's what happened about a week ago," Kim said. "He had finished the job and I'd gotten the key back from him, but then I caught him in the Pullman one afternoon. I asked him what he was doing in there and how he got in, and he said he was just checking on a light fixture and that he'd gotten the key from the front desk. But when I asked around, no one would admit giving it to him." She sighed. "I just wish this was all over."

"What a nightmare," Janet said.

"It is," Kim said. "But hopefully we'll win the lawsuit and he'll have to pay for the extra costs instead of the other way around."

"I wish I'd known it was happening." Not that Janet could have done anything about it.

"It's okay," Kim said. "You didn't know, because I didn't want you to. This whole thing reflects poorly on the museum and the Pullman. Who would want to rent it out if they knew the work was such poor quality? We really didn't want to sue him. We tried to work it out without it coming to this, but he flatly refused to negotiate. So we've been trying to keep the whole thing quiet. Patricia has been wonderful. She's pretty sure we'll win the case when it goes to court."

Janet supposed she should have guessed that the suit was going to court if its evidence had been in the warehouse. What else would it be doing there if it wasn't awaiting trial? And it made sense that Patricia was the lawyer representing the depot.

Kim's mouth formed a grim line. "Todd has refused to settle unless we pay him the exorbitant fee he's asking for, which is not going to happen. We don't even have that much in our annual budget."

"I'm sorry for all the trouble this has caused you."

"Thank you." Kim gave a small smile. "We're hoping it'll be resolved soon."

Janet hoped so too. But if there had been evidence against Todd in the warehouse that burned, the resolution might not go the museum's way. Ian's list had said something about upholstery and something electrical. "Did you hear about the fire at the warehouse the other night?"

"Yes, I did. What a disaster."

"Ian said the museum had some things stored there," Janet said.

"The museum had a little corner the space. Some old displays and things like that. Nothing we couldn't afford to lose, though it's still sad for me because I feel connected to our items and their history. I am concerned about the evidence we had against Todd in the police section of the warehouse. Patricia told me it's likely the evidence that was there is gone, though she doesn't know for sure yet. Maybe something survived. For now, I'm going to focus on making the festival a success."

Janet doubted that any evidence had survived based on what Ian had told her, but she didn't say so. Kim didn't need her hopes dashed. "I think that's a great attitude, Kim."

"We're so sorry about all of this," Debbie said again.

Janet and Debbie waved goodbye, and then they got into Debbie's car and started toward Janet's house so they could pick up Ian's donation clothes before they headed over to the Wilsons' house.

"So it sounds like Todd did subpar work and cut corners," Debbie said.

"And he used the money the museum gave him for the Pullman to pay off debts on his other projects instead of buying quality materials."

"But he has such a great reputation, according to Kim."

"And according to his website," Janet said. "Though obviously that would only reflect the positive."

"How has he collected a stellar roster of clients and created such a strong portfolio if he was crooked the whole time?" Debbie asked.

"I don't know," Janet said. "If what Kim is saying is right, the museum can't possibly be the first unhappy customer he's had."

"We should try to find out if he's been sued before."

"Good idea," Janet said. "Though that won't tell us whether he set fire to the warehouse to get rid of the evidence."

"No," Debbie agreed. "It won't."

Janet knew Ian was probably already checking Todd's business history. He didn't need her help solving this crime. But this was Kim and the Dennison Depot Museum. The café and the museum were different entities, but they fed one another. If someone had cheated the museum, it affected the café too. Especially if they were talking about the Pullman, which brought in overnight guests who needed to eat. And since she'd already found a couple of clues in relation to the café, she was invested.

"I guess we'll need to see if we can find out more about him," Janet said.

CHAPTER EIGHT

A few minutes later, they arrived at Janet's house, where they loaded up two trash bags full of Ian's old clothes. Then they headed over to the Wilsons' house, which stood among a stretch of cute bungalows in an older section of town. They hauled the trash bags to the porch and knocked on the door.

Carrie opened it, and her face broke into a wide grin. "Hello." Around their age, she had brown hair with a few streaks of gray and the prettiest green eyes. "How nice to see you both. Those must be the clothes for the drive. Thank you so much."

"We also brought cookies." Debbie held out the bag she'd filled before they left the café.

"Well, aren't you sweet? Please, come in." Carrie stepped back to let them in, and the air inside the house felt cool and pleasant after the hot oven of the July afternoon. She led them into an entryway, where jackets and sweaters hung on hooks and shoes and athletic bags lay on the floor. One bag was long enough to hold baseball bats, and Janet could see cleats peeking out of another. Beyond the entryway was a living room with hardwood floors, soft area rugs, and blue-and-white couches and chairs. "I'll take those and be right back."

Carrie managed to grab both garbage bags and the bag of cookies and carry them out of the room.

While she was gone, Janet studied the display on the mantel. Framed photos of Tyler in his high school baseball uniform lined the wooden shelf and sat amongst trophies and medals. A framed certificate from Crackerjack Bats hung on the wall over the mantel, sharing the frame with a photo of Tyler holding a bat. The logo on the bat faced the camera. It was a Crackerjack bat, which made sense when she realized that the certificate was a sponsorship agreement.

Actually, now that she was close, she could see that Tyler held a Crackerjack bat in every photo. She didn't follow baseball, but she didn't think it was one of the better-known brands for baseball gear. The fact that they were a smaller company was probably why they had been willing to sponsor a high school student.

Carrie returned a few minutes later with the cookies on a plate. "Would you like to sit for a moment?" She gestured toward the sofa. "I have some fresh lemonade in the fridge."

"That sounds lovely," Janet said.

Carrie ducked out of the room once more as Debbie sat down on the couch.

Janet continued to study the display over the mantel. Every photo, trophy, and certificate was related to Tyler and baseball. It must have been disorienting when his injury sidelined his career. Judging by what she saw, his baseball participation was everything to this family.

"Here we are," Carrie said, returning with a tray that held frosty glasses of lemonade. She set it down on the coffee table, and Janet walked to the couch.

"Did Tyler enjoy the gum and the candy?" Debbie asked.

"He was so tickled," Carrie said. "I think he's eaten half of the Necco wafers and all of the peanut candy already."

"That's good stuff," Debbie said. "What about the gum?"

"He unwrapped a piece the minute I handed it to him," Carrie said. "He loves it, which I will never understand."

Janet had been hoping Carrie would reveal more, but she wasn't sure what. It seemed unlikely she would admit or even know if Tyler had chewed gum at the site of the warehouse fire. Janet decided to try another angle.

"You must be so proud of him," she said, gesturing toward the display.

"Yes, we are, of course," Carrie said. "But he's had a string of rotten luck, and it's been a tough couple of years for him."

"Janet said he had an injury," Debbie said, picking up a glass.

"That's right," Carrie said. "He was an all-star high school athlete and played in the High School World Series. He had such a strong career in front of him. His batting average was the highest in the state. We were so proud when he got a scholarship to Ohio State. A full ride—can you believe it? And he loved life at college. But during a game against Indiana his sophomore year, he tore his ACL sliding into second. He missed the rest of that season, and when it took him longer to recover than the university thought it should, they dropped him. He lost his scholarship and then his sponsorship, and that was that."

"I'm so sorry to hear that," Debbie said. "That's terrible. How is he doing now?"

"Much better, thank you. But without the scholarship, getting a college education is tough. He's working on getting back into shape, and I know he'll try out for other schools as soon as he can. But in the meantime, he's here, and it's been challenging for him. We're hoping he'll get into the right program in time for the spring season."

"He's an amazing player," Janet said. "Any school would be lucky to have him."

"I agree. He just needs to believe in himself and make it happen."

"We'll pray for him," Debbie said.

"Thank you," Carrie said. "Tell you what, if you're going to pray for him, you may as well add something else to the list. He was doing some delivery driving to help out while he's figuring things out. But he had an accident a few months back, and the police are accusing him of drinking and driving. I—" Carrie broke off and seemed to realize who she was talking to. "I'm sorry, Janet. I know this isn't Ian's doing. Please don't take offense."

"None taken," she said, keeping her face neutral. She considered Carrie a friend, but criticism of the police was difficult for her to hear.

"The thing is, I know he wouldn't do that. He's a smart kid and a good boy. He wouldn't risk his future like that. We raised him better than that. And they have no proof, so the whole thing is silly. But they've suspended his license, and he can't do his job without that, obviously. It just seems like they were looking for something to accuse him of."

Debbie met Janet's eye, and Janet could see that her friend was as mystified by Carrie's words as she was. The reason the police didn't have proof that Tyler had been drinking and driving was that he'd refused a breath test. That was why his license had been suspended. It was a direct result of his noncooperation and not because the police "were looking for something to accuse him of." Did Carrie truly not understand that? They'd done field sobriety tests, which he'd evidently failed, and there had been beer cans found in his car.

"It has to be hard for him," Debbie said, managing to convey a sympathetic tone that Janet couldn't quite bring herself to muster. "To have his dream crushed in the blink of an eye like that. Of course he's struggling."

"It's been hard," Carrie said, nodding. "But we'll get through this."

Schooling her tone and expression, Janet asked, "What is Tyler up to these days? Is he able to get out much?" She hadn't heard or seen him at the house, if he was there.

"He's been mowing lawns this summer and got himself a part-time job stocking shelves at the grocery store," Carrie said. "He can walk to it, so that's helpful. Hopefully, after the case goes to trial, he'll be able to put this behind him and get his old life back."

"I hope his trial isn't delayed because of that fire earlier this week," Debbie said.

Janet shot her a look. She hadn't intended to mention the fire. But Debbie didn't meet her eye.

"The one at the warehouse?" Carrie said. "I heard about that. Tyler was at a movie that night and said the traffic was really bad getting back because of it. But why would that delay the trial?"

If she was acting, she was good. She genuinely seemed not to understand. But did that mean Tyler—or Austin—was ignorant of what had been in the warehouse? One of them could have set the fire without Carrie's knowledge.

"The warehouse is shared by several departments," Janet explained. "It's where the police department stores evidence. From what we understand, some of the evidence they had there was damaged or destroyed."

"That's too bad," Carrie said. "But it better not delay his case. He needs these charges dismissed so he can move on with his life."

Janet was surprised at Carrie's reaction to destroyed evidence, but then she considered how she would feel if it were Tiffany instead of Tyler. Carrie's reaction wasn't that far from what her own might be.

"Do they know what started the fire?" Carrie asked.

Janet assumed her questions meant that Ian and his team hadn't questioned Tyler about the fire yet, so she wanted to be careful what she said.

"I'm sure the police are exploring every possibility," she said.

"Well, I hope they figure it out, but mostly I hope it doesn't delay the trial."

"You said Tyler was out on Tuesday night," Debbie said. "What movie? I hear the new superhero movie isn't as good as the previous ones in the franchise. I've been trying to decide whether to go see it or not."

Janet was pretty sure Debbie wasn't a big fan of superhero movies but was impressed by how convincing she sounded.

"That was it. It was the new superhero movie. He went with his cousin Rex. He said it was good."

"I heard it's really long," Debbie said.

"I don't know. They went to the seven-thirty showing. Rex picked him up at seven, and he didn't come home until around eleven. I don't know if they did anything after the movie or not."

That was assuming he actually went to the theater. Janet didn't know the exact time the fire had started, but she and Ian had gotten out of Bible study around eight, so she assumed the fire started shortly before then.

"Maybe I'll give it a shot," Debbie said. "But I'll have to go to an earlier show. I can't stay up that late." She looked around. "Austin must pull crazy hours at the hospital. Does he ever have to work nights?"

"He works days, nights—you name it. I don't know how he does it. My body wouldn't be able to deal with so much change. But he's always been able to sleep anywhere, anytime, so he's able to roll with it."

"I'm so jealous of people like that," Janet said. "I have to have a routine."

"Me too," Debbie said. "It must be nice to be that flexible." She took a sip of her lemonade and then said, "Hey, no one was hurt in the warehouse fire, were they? Did Austin say anyone came to the hospital with injuries?"

If Carrie hadn't seen through their questions by now, she definitely would with that one. But she was still smiling.

"Austin was at work on Tuesday night, but he works in the children's wing, so he probably wouldn't know about that."

"That makes sense," Debbie said.

Janet knew it was time to change the subject, before Carrie figured out why they were really there, if she hadn't already.

"Tell me about that painting behind you." Janet indicated the painting of sand dunes studded with seagrass leading up to a sandy beach and turquoise water.

Carrie beamed and started talking about a trip to South Carolina and how they'd purchased the artwork to remember the trip. Debbie told Carrie about her own visit to the beaches of South Carolina several years before. They chatted for a while longer. Then Janet and Debbie thanked Carrie for her hospitality, wished her luck with the clothing drive, and headed out the door.

"I thought we weren't going to talk about the fire," Janet said when they were back in the car and the vents were pumping out cold air.

"I didn't plan on it. It kind of slipped out."

Janet pressed her lips together. She really didn't want to interfere in the investigation. But she had to admit, she was interested to know what Tyler and Austin had been up to that night. Though the police would also be checking alibis.

"Either Tyler is being unfairly maligned, or Carrie is in serious denial about her son," Debbie said.

"She might not have the clearest picture of her son's behavior," Janet said carefully.

"I think that's a very kind way of saying it." Debbie put the car in gear and pulled away from the curb. "She seems to believe he's totally innocent. I'm not a parent, so I have no experience with this, but I would think that when the police say he was driving under the influence, she might want to consider the possibility that it's true. Regardless of what she wants to believe about how she raised him."

"Or at least consider that his refusal to take a breath test is cause for suspicion," Janet agreed. "But that doesn't tell us anything about whether he had anything to do with the warehouse fire. Or whether his father did either."

"Carrie said Austin was at work. I assume the police will verify that," Debbie said. "The hospital wouldn't tell us one way or the other, but we could find out if there really was a superhero movie playing at the theater at seven thirty on Tuesday. That wouldn't prove that

Tyler was at the theater, but it would at least tell us whether his alibi is plausible. Do you have time to swing by?"

"Are you sure you're not itching to see the movie yourself? You sounded very convincing in there."

Debbie laughed. "Superhero movies are not my thing, sadly. Give me a good Jane Austen adaptation any time. We can see if one of those is playing instead."

Janet grinned. "Okay. Let's go."

CHAPTER NINE

John set his heavy bag on the train platform. Mama
had wanted to come see him off, but he'd insisted on
saying his goodbyes back at the house. He couldn't let
his last glimpse of Mama be of her crying on the train
platform. He already knew he was breaking her heart
by leaving like this—she'd told him so a hundred times.
She thought he wasn't going to come home alive.

The trees were heavy with orange leaves, and the sky
was a piercing blue. The tracks began to rattle, and he
craned his neck and saw the train coming down the line.
It slowed as it approached the station, hissing and belch-
ing smoke and a sour, metallic smell. He stepped back.

"John." It was Vernon Franklin's father, Harry,
who always wore a blue-checked tie at church. Now he
wore a porter's cap and uniform, and he smiled as he

approached John on the platform. John had thought he was a conductor. How had he gotten himself demoted to porter, which any teen could do? "So this is it."

"It is." John was counting down the minutes.

"You're doing such a brave thing, stepping up to serve like this. We'll all be praying for you to come home to us safely."

Afterward, John didn't know what made him say it. Maybe it was the emotion of hugging his mama goodbye earlier. Maybe it was the way the preacher had called him up to the front of the church so they could all pray for him yesterday. Maybe it was too many years in this dumpy little town among people who were content to accept the way things were. People who weren't forward-thinking enough to see that the world was changing, that a better life was possible.

But whatever the reason, instead of simply thanking Mr. Franklin and getting on the train, John faced him and said what he'd held inside for so long. "I won't be coming back."

"What?" Mr. Franklin's eyes widened. "What do you mean, son?" The train slowed as it moved closer, its brakes screeching.

"Even if I survive this war, I won't ever return. I can't stay here, surrounded by people who are willing to accept whatever terrible circumstances they were born into. I may not be able to afford college, but I will never settle for being a porter, or a janitor, or a line worker in a factory. I could never be content with that pathetic kind of life."

Mr. Franklin frowned and opened his mouth to say something, but now that John had gotten started, he couldn't stop.

"The world has changed. The civil rights movement is not going away. That preacher Dr. King is making them pay attention. And I, for one, will not sit here in a backwater town, cleaning up after other people when I could be out there making something of myself. So no, I won't be returning to Dennison. I'd rather get shot in Vietnam than end up a poor old porter, hoisting bags for people who don't even care that I exist."

Mr. Franklin blinked, but before he could say anything, the train roared into the station, and as soon as the doors opened, John picked up his bag and stepped on.

He hoped he never saw this miserable train station ever again.

Debbie turned onto the road that led to the shopping center in New Philadelphia. The movie theater was tucked into the back, and they drove around for a few minutes to find a parking spot.

"A lot of people must be anxious to escape the heat here," Debbie said.

"Not a bad idea on a summer day," Janet said.

They finally parked and walked to the theater, and Janet scanned the showtimes. There was an animated film, an action movie, a remake of some eighties film—and a movie about some kind of superhero. She couldn't begin to guess what his power was from the muscle-bound figure on the poster.

"I guess we just ask the guy selling tickets what the showtimes were for Tuesday night," she said.

"Let's go." Debbie pulled the door open and stepped inside.

The air felt blessedly cool and smelled of popcorn and sugar. Janet immediately wanted buttered popcorn. It was impossible to resist that smell. They crossed the garishly patterned carpet and walked toward the ticket booth.

"How can I help you?" asked the teenage boy behind the glass.

"We were wondering if you could tell us what times that super-hero movie played on Tuesday," Debbie said.

Confusion crossed his freckled face. "You don't want to buy a ticket for today?"

"No thank you," Debbie said. "Just hoping to find out the times for Tuesday's show."

"One second." He typed something into the computer on the counter in front of him. "It played at one, four thirty, and eight."

"Not at seven thirty?" Janet asked.

He peered at the screen, clearly double-checking. "No, ma'am. Not on Tuesday."

"Thank you very much," Debbie told him.

"Is there anything else I can help you with?" he asked. "I know you said you're not seeing a movie today, but if you're interested, I can still sign you up for a loyalty pass. If you see ten movies, you get to see an eleventh for free."

"Not today, thank you." Debbie smiled and thanked him again, and they headed back outside. The heat hit Janet like an electric blanket on the highest setting.

"There was no show at seven thirty," she said. "So Tyler was lying."

"Or his mom got it wrong," Debbie said. "Or she was lying."

"Could he have shown up early for the one at eight?" Janet asked, but it sounded like a stretch as she said it.

"His mom said he was home by eleven, so I guess that would be theoretically possible if it was a short movie and there were no previews at the beginning."

"But we know it was a long movie. And there are always previews."

"So something about his story is off," Debbie said.

"And I'm sure Ian and his team will discover what it is."

"I'm sure you're right," Debbie said as they climbed into the car. "Here's a question. Tyler isn't allowed to drive right now. How would he have been able to get to the warehouse to start the fire?"

"Maybe he got a ride?" Janet suggested. "If his cousin picked him up Tuesday night, they could have been in on it together. Or maybe Tyler drove anyway. Just because he's not legally allowed to drive doesn't mean he didn't. No one is legally allowed to commit arson, but someone did."

"Fair enough," Debbie said. "But Tyler isn't the only suspect." She started the engine, and blessedly cool air streamed out of the vents. "Neither is Austin. Maybe we could find out where some of the others were Tuesday night."

"I don't think so," Janet said. "Going to see Carrie was one thing. We had to drop the clothes off at her house anyway. But I don't think we should start showing up at the homes of other suspects."

"What if we show up at a house they don't live in?" Debbie suggested.

"What do you mean?"

"You said one of the suspects had been arrested for arson, for burning down a house she'd inherited. It couldn't hurt anything to go check that out, could it?"

"Why would we do that?" Janet asked.

"I don't know. Maybe seeing it in person would help us make more sense of what happened there. Maybe there would be a clear connection to the warehouse in the way both buildings burned or something." Debbie adjusted her vent. "And since no one lives there, we won't be upsetting anyone. We can go take a peek."

Janet wasn't sure it was a good idea, but she didn't have an indisputable reason for why they shouldn't. After all, the house wasn't part of an active investigation, so they probably wouldn't be stepping on the police department's toes if they went. She doubted they would be able to tell much about the burn patterns of the fires, given that they had zero training. If there was a connection, the fire inspector would certainly work that out. But maybe there would be some other clue connecting the two crime scenes. Another gum wrapper, or receipt, or—she didn't know. She couldn't deny being curious.

"All right," she finally said. "I don't see how we could do any damage by driving by the site of the house Jennie burned down."

"The house she *allegedly* burned down," Debbie corrected.

"Fine. Allegedly."

"Awesome. Where is it?" She put the car in gear and looked at Janet expectantly.

"I don't remember the address. Let me find it." Janet pulled up the *Gazette* newspaper website on her phone and found the article about the fire she'd read before. "Here it is. 548 Clasp Hollow Road."

Debbie typed the address into her GPS app. "It's a fifteen-minute drive."

"That's not too bad."

"You can tell me more about the fire on the way."

As Debbie drove, Janet read her the newspaper article. Then she recapped the details about how the house had fallen into disrepair and passed to Jennie after her mother's death.

"How long after it officially became Jennie's problem did it burn down?" Debbie asked.

"A couple of months," Janet said. "Long enough for her to take out a large insurance policy on it."

"That's convenient."

"The police thought so as well."

Soon they were driving down Clasp Hollow Road. Debbie slowed as Janet scanned the numbers on the mailboxes. It was a small rural road that snaked its way along a dry creek bed. The houses were spaced far apart, and there was an interesting mix of newer ranches and older farmhouses, including a couple of pretty Victorians. There were also a few very dilapidated properties, some of which had junk cars and old appliances in the yards. Trees and patches of woods surrounded several of the houses, while others stood on land that had been cleared completely for farming.

"It's right up there," Janet said, pointing to a mailbox at the end of a rutted dirt driveway. The house itself wasn't visible from the road, but Janet spotted it set back amongst trees as they crept up the drive. What was left of the house—a blackened shell of a structure—was surrounded by a clearing, with trees on all sides and a yard choked with weeds. It had once been a two-story home, judging by the section of wall that still stood and half a charred staircase.

"There's not much left," Debbie said, stepping out of the car.

"It probably took quite a while for the fire trucks to make it all this way," Janet said. "Thank goodness no one was living here at the time, so there were no injuries."

It hadn't been a small house, judging by the footprint and the height of the remaining wall. There was a hint of chimney smell, but it was mixed with the scent of milkweed and the pine trees around the clearing. At the side of the house, an overgrown garden was surrounded by a chicken-wire fence, and roses and purple coneflowers blossomed despite being choked with weeds.

"It must have been a nice house once," Janet murmured.

"It's sad that it came to this." Debbie started walking toward the wrecked shell.

"Be careful," Janet said. "I doubt that structure is sound in any way."

"I will be," Debbie promised. She slowly walked the perimeter of the place.

Janet followed a step behind her, looking for…she didn't even know what. Some clue or sign that would point to the fact that the person who had set this fire was the same one who had set the fire at the warehouse.

When they made it back to the car, Debbie shrugged. "It's a shame."

"It is," Janet agreed. "But I don't see anything that helps with the warehouse."

"Me neither." Debbie reached for the door handle.

As Janet reached for hers, a pickup truck wheeled off the road and bumped its way up the driveway.

"Who's that?" Debbie asked.

"Your guess is as good as mine."

The truck stopped behind Debbie's car, and a woman with short blond hair stepped out. She wore knee-length camo-print shorts, combat boots, and a shirt with a logo from a popular brand of hunting clothing. It was Jennie Ward. Janet recognized her from the photos on her social media.

"Who are you, and what are you doing here?" she demanded.

"Hi." Janet put on her best innocent smile and turned so the woman could see that her T-shirt read I CAN'T. I HAVE COOKIES TO BAKE. She hoped that it showed Jennie they weren't a threat. "My name is Janet Shaw, and this is my friend Debbie Albright. I'm sorry if we've disturbed you."

"This is private property," she said, stepping toward them.

"We're so sorry." Debbie used her sweetest voice too. "We'll get out of your way."

"What do you want? Who sent you?"

"No one," Janet said. "We—"

"I know this place looks abandoned, but I have motion-detecting cameras," Jennie said. "They alert me when people come onto my property."

Janet realized she'd seen Jennie before—and not just on social media. But where?

"That's a very smart idea," Debbie said.

"Who sent you?"

Where had Janet seen her? Had there been a photo of Jennie in the newspaper? She didn't think so.

"Nobody," Debbie said again.

"We thought this was interesting," Janet added. "We didn't know we'd be disturbing anyone. We'll go."

Jennie appraised them for a long moment then stepped back, and they quickly climbed into the car. Jennie got in her truck and pulled over, waiting for them to exit the property, and when Debbie got on the road, Jennie followed them for nearly a mile before she turned into another driveway.

It wasn't until then that Janet remembered. "She was at the fire."

"What?"

"The warehouse fire. A lot of people stood around, watching, and she was one of them. I saw her there." She'd been in the crowd that Brendan and Ethan had kept back.

"Are you sure?"

"Positive." Janet remembered her short blond hair and big eyes. "I didn't pay any attention to her at the time because I didn't know who she was, but having seen her now, yes. I'm sure. She was there."

"Don't they say arsonists like to see their work?" Debbie said.

"I suppose so, but Ian said lots of people were there to watch. They didn't all set the fire."

"But one of them might have. And arson does seem to be her thing."

"Allegedly," Janet reminded her. "And her being at the fire is not proof of anything."

"No, it's not," Debbie said. "Which means we have to keep digging."

CHAPTER TEN

Ian didn't make it home for dinner Thursday night. Janet was used to him having to work long hours on big cases, but she couldn't say she was always happy about it. Throughout dinner, Tiffany chattered away about a prank she and her roommates had pulled on the girls in another suite in their dorm, but Janet was lost with all the names. So many other people were a part of Tiffany's life now, and Janet didn't know most of them.

After dinner, Tiffany said she was heading out again.

"Don't stay out too late," Janet said.

"I won't. By the way, Hudson confirmed the cabin for that weekend after we get back from the lake."

"Okay." Something in the way Tiffany said it made Janet think she wasn't as excited about the weekend as she had been the last time they'd talked about it. "You're sure you want to go?"

"Yeah," Tiffany said, her gaze on the floor. "I do."

Janet believed her. But there was still something in her manner that said otherwise.

"Let me know if there's anything you need," she finally said.

"I will." Tiffany hesitated and then added, "Thanks, Mom."

Janet watched her walk out, unsettled. Tiffany's friends were good kids. They would be fine in a cabin on a lake for a weekend.

But was Tiffany unsure about it for some reason? It was hard to know how much to push her daughter for answers. She had to trust Tiffany to make good decisions, but she also wanted to be available if Tiffany needed advice. Should she remind her of that? Where was the line between helping and meddling?

She thought longingly of the good old days at the lake again. Those days were so blessedly uncomplicated.

Janet intended to go to bed relatively early to make up for how little sleep she'd gotten the night before. But before she turned in, she wanted to do more research into Todd Mills. She decided to visit the clerk of courts website again and see if she could find records for the suit the depot had filed against Todd Mills. She sat down at the table and opened her laptop to get started. Ranger got up from his spot on the couch and rubbed against her legs, purring. She scooped him up and set him on her lap, where he curled up, still purring.

She searched for *depot museum* and easily found the complaint that had been filed against Mills Contracting and Renovation by the Dennison Depot Museum. The lawyer who had filed the suit on behalf of the depot was Patricia Franklin, as she'd expected.

Janet read the complaint carefully, trying to work through the complex legalese. From what she could tell, Todd was accused of defrauding the depot of more than $20,000 for supplies they'd paid him for but that had never materialized. He was also accused of gross negligence and breach of contract. From what Kim had said, Janet knew that Todd had refused to admit guilt or to settle, so the case was scheduled to be brought to trial later in the summer.

That was interesting enough, but it didn't tell her anything she didn't already know. She clicked back to the search page. This time she entered *Mills Contracting and Renovation*, and several hits came up.

The first one was a suit that had been brought against Todd by the owners of the Moonlight Historic Inn for breach of contract and fraud the previous year. Apparently, he had taken money from the project and failed to produce the promised materials, regularly missed deadlines, and failed to finish the work so the required permits could be closed out. Todd had settled that case, paying $30,000 to the plaintiffs—far below what the suit claimed he owed them.

She clicked back to the search results and found a similar suit filed by the owners of the Bedford S. Jamison House and Museum. They had hired him to transform the house, which had once belonged to a minor figure in the Ohio legislature, into a museum.

How did Todd keep getting hired for projects with such a record?

But how would a potential client know about the lawsuits? He certainly didn't advertise them, and his website boasted of happy clients and their reviews. Still, it seemed odd that word hadn't gotten around among the contractors in the area and tradespeople he worked with, and from those people to potential clients. Unless he paid for their silence.

Janet shook her head. Now she was inventing conspiracies. But she felt it was unfair that he was still in business. He couldn't keep going out and taking clients' money only to deliver shoddy work.

Had he set fire to the warehouse to hide the evidence against him in the depot lawsuit? She wasn't ruling it out, though she thought it less likely than some of the other scenarios. Burning down a warehouse to cover up evidence of arson or drunk driving or whatever had gotten Jedidiah Merrick in trouble seemed far more likely than this civil case.

Janet was exhausted, so she headed up to bed and fell into a deep, dreamless sleep. She was dead to the world until something startled her awake. She shot up and reached over to the other side of the bed. Ian wasn't there. She glanced at the clock. It was a quarter after eleven. What had awakened her?

She crept out of bed and flipped on the hallway light. Nothing. Slowly, quietly, she made her way through the house. The kitchen light was on.

"Did I wake you?" Ian looked at her sheepishly as she walked into the room. "I dropped my water bottle."

"I'm glad that's all it was."

"I'm so sorry I woke you."

"It's okay. I'm glad you're home." Janet stretched her arms over her head. "Is Tiffany back too?"

Ian nodded. "She came in a few minutes ago and went right up to bed."

"I'm glad she made it home."

Ian's laptop was open on the table, beside a plate that held the remains of a microwave burrito.

"Why don't you come to bed?" she asked.

"I would love to," Ian said. "But as soon as I walked in the door, I got a call that the security camera footage from the warehouse had come in."

"Can you see anything useful on it?"

"No, sadly. I mean, you can see some stuff, but it's not clear." The frozen image on his screen showed a person in baggy black clothing wearing a ski mask. In spite of the July temperatures, the person wore a heavy jacket and gloves, which made it impossible to even tell the gender.

"Can I watch it?"

She fully expected Ian to say no, but he surprised her by starting the video over. At first, all the camera showed was the ground and the side and door of the warehouse. Aside from a few moths flitting around in the beam from a floodlight, nothing moved.

But then a person came into the frame. They kept their face down, but they moved purposefully, directly toward the camera. Janet was so focused on trying to make out who it was that she didn't see the baseball bat in their hand until it swung directly at the camera. In a split second, the bat hit the camera lens, which shattered, and then the screen went black.

"Wait. Can I see that again?"

Ian replayed the footage.

Janet waited until the bat was in full view. "Pause it, please."

Ian pressed the space bar, and the footage froze on the screen.

And that was when Janet saw it. "That's the logo for Crackerjack Bats."

"What?"

"The baseball bat company. It's right there on the bat. See?" She pointed to the black squiggle that she knew was the logo.

Ian squinted at the screen. He opened a browser tab and searched *Crackerjack Bats*. The company's website came up with the logo prominently displayed.

"Wow. How did you know that?"

"I went to drop off your old clothes for the clothing drive at the Wilsons' house. Carrie had asked me to bring them by ahead of the drive, so I took them over today, and Debbie and I visited with her for a while. Their whole mantel is full of stuff about Tyler's baseball career, and there are lots of pictures of him with Crackerjack bats. He was sponsored by them."

"He was?" Ian raised an eyebrow.

"He was a big-shot baseball player in high school. You knew that."

"I knew that, but I didn't realize he had a sponsorship."

"I mean, it's not one of the most famous bat companies, but it's still a pretty big deal."

"I'd say so," Ian said.

"In every photo of him I saw at their house, he was holding a Crackerjack bat," Janet said. "That doesn't mean it was him, necessarily. But put that together with the gum wrapper that was found at the site of the fire, and—well, it just doesn't look too good for Tyler right now."

"It's a good tip about the bat."

Janet was glad Ian was pleased. She didn't want to push her luck, but she thought she should tell him what else she knew. "As we were chatting, Carrie told us that Tyler went to see that new superhero movie on the night of the fire. She said it was a seven-thirty show, but there wasn't a seven-thirty showing of that movie on Tuesday night."

"I haven't been by to speak to Tyler yet. I hope you didn't suggest to his mother that he was a suspect?"

"No." Janet shook her head. "Absolutely not."

"Okay." He gave her a weary smile.

Should she tell him about seeing Jennie at the fire? She didn't want to upset him. But it did seem like a detail that the police needed to know. Would it be worse if she withheld that information, or if she told him what she'd learned?

"Also, Jennie Ward was at the fire," she blurted before she could change her mind. "I saw her there that night."

"How would you have recognized her?"

"Her social media page has her picture all over it," Janet said. "Plus, Debbie and I went out to the site of the fire at her mom's place. We wanted to see it. We weren't planning on talking to anyone or touching anything. But apparently, she has motion-activated cameras on the property, and she came over and asked us to leave."

"Janet—" he began.

"I know. We shouldn't have been there. I'm sorry, Ian. I never thought it would go down the way it did. We shouldn't have gone in the first place."

"You're right," Ian said. "You shouldn't have." But after a moment, he added, "But when you saw her, you recognized her from the warehouse fire?"

"She was there," Janet said. "She was by Brendan. Ask him if he remembers her."

"Believe me, I will." Ian made another note in his notebook. "Is that all, or can we talk about something other than the case so I might actually be able to sleep tonight?"

Janet considered his request, then said, "I'm making shopping lists for things we need for the trip to the cabin. Is there anything you want to add?"

"That's right. I forgot about that."

"You forgot about the trip?" It had been on the kitchen calendar for months. She'd been talking about it for weeks.

"I didn't forget about the trip entirely." His voice was apologetic. "I just didn't realize it was coming up so soon."

"It'll be a good break. You need some time away."

"With everything going on, Janet, I don't know if I will be able to get away."

"What? You still have a week until we leave. Surely you'll figure out who set the fire before then."

"Even if we do, there'll be a lot of work dealing with the cases where the evidence was destroyed. It's kind of a nightmare. I don't know if things will have settled down by then."

"You want to cancel the trip?" Janet couldn't believe it.

"No, no," Ian said immediately. "You and Tiffany should still go. I don't know if I'll be able to get away, but that doesn't mean you two shouldn't get to enjoy it."

"It's a family vacation. We can't leave a third of the family behind."

"I don't want you two to miss out," Ian insisted. "I know how much you've been looking forward to this. You guys should still go."

Janet felt tears prick her eyes. How could he even think about not coming? They'd been counting down to this for months. It was their first trip together since Tiffany left for college. It was their chance to relax as a family and recreate memories from simpler days. And now he wasn't going to come?

"I'm sorry, Janet." Ian's voice had softened. "It's not that I don't want to be there. Believe me—I want nothing more than to leave all this behind. But with the fire, I don't see how I could get away. I have an obligation to the public. Think how it would look if I left on a vacation without a suspect in custody or with loose ends from the other cases still out there."

"I understand." Or at least, she was trying to. She'd long known that being married to a police officer meant that the good of the public often came before the good of the family. It was a fact she'd reconciled herself to years ago. But he'd never done something like cancel or skip a family vacation for a case before. Though she understood why this case was such a big deal, it still hurt.

"I know how excited you are about it," Ian said. "And you and Tiff could use some girl time, right?"

Janet bit her tongue. She didn't want to speak until she was sure she could control the tone of her voice. Girl time with Tiffany would be nice. Finally, after a few deep breaths, she said, "If you were able to solve the case quickly and wrap up the loose ends before the trip, would you be able to come then?"

Ian let out a long breath. "Probably. I mean, if we had this thing locked up, that would go a long way."

Challenge accepted. If solving the case was the only way he'd get to come on the family vacation, well then, she would do everything she could to make sure the case was solved.

CHAPTER ELEVEN

Vietnam
1966

Dear Mama,

Thank you for your letter. It's always nice to have news from home. I'm glad Nicky is happy, though I still can't see what he likes about Sherry. And I hope Seelie is doing better. Those kids were running her ragged last I saw.

It's so hot here. I thought Ohio was hot, but this place is on a whole different level. The food is good though. I didn't see much of Saigon, but if I get to go back, I'll send you a postcard. We're mostly spending time on the base, but we've made some forays into the jungle. It's beautiful but also really dangerous, they tell us.

The other guys are nice enough. There are people here from all over. My bunkmate is from New Orleans and has the thickest accent. I can't understand him half the time, but he's a good guy.

Regarding your thoughts about my conversation with Mr. Franklin, I probably shouldn't have even told you about it. I'm sorry I said what I said to him, but I can't say I didn't mean it. I'm sorry if that's not what you wanted to hear, but it's true. I couldn't stay in Dennison and become someone like him. How can he stand there and smile all day while folks ignore him and treat him like he's not there? He can do better than that, Mama. Maybe if he starts to expect more, he'll get more.

They're calling us to dinner. I've got to go.

John

Janet knew Friday would be a busy day with the festival starting in the afternoon. As she drove to work and set about getting the first batch of goodies in the oven, she prayed for God's blessing on the day, on the people she would encounter, and on the veterans who had served their country. She asked the Lord to bring the people into her path that He wanted her to encourage and that she would serve Him well.

So she wasn't surprised when the first customer of the day was the same veteran who had shown up in search of Harry on Wednesday. Today he wore a short-sleeve button-down with a small pin that said VETERAN, as well as a baseball cap that said ARMY.

"Hello, John," Janet greeted him. "Welcome back."

"Thank you. This is the best coffee in town."

"I'm glad you feel that way," Janet said. "Another cup of brewed, black?"

"Good memory. To go, please."

"Sure thing." She waved away the bills he offered her. "It's on us. Thank you for your service."

"It was an honor to serve my country."

"Are you from this area originally?" She plucked a to-go cup from the stack and took it to the carafe.

"Yes indeed. Dennison, born and bred. I joined up during Vietnam and served overseas. After I made it back to the States, I moved to Cincinnati. Been there ever since, though I'm in town now for a few weeks to help my mom. She had a fall."

"I'm sorry to hear that." Rich coffee splashed into the cup. "Though I'm glad you've returned for a while."

"It's nice to be here," he said. "I was worried this place would bring back too many memories, and it does but not in the way I thought."

"In a good way or a bad way?"

"I haven't decided yet. It's not how I remembered it, that's for sure."

She finished filling the cup and snapped a plastic lid on it. "Did you end up finding Harry?"

Something passed over his face, something Janet couldn't read. "Not yet," he said. "I didn't make it in here yesterday. Mama wasn't feeling well, so I stayed with her."

"I'm sorry to hear that."

"Thank you. She's doing much better today."

"Who is your mother?" Janet didn't know everyone in town, but she'd at least heard of most people.

"Edna Milken."

Janet set the coffee in front of him. "She worked at the hospital, right? Sings in the choir at her church?" Edna didn't go to Faith Community, but Janet had met her when she'd come to lead special music a few years back. She'd sung so beautifully and with so much heart that it had stayed with Janet for weeks afterward.

"That's right. You know her?"

"I've met her. I'm sorry to hear she's not doing well."

"She's a tough woman. She'll pull through."

"I'll be praying for her."

"Thank you."

She wiped down the counter, which was already clean. "So you're not here for the festival, then?"

"That's a coincidence," he said. "But it's nice to see how this place still celebrates veterans. That's one thing it's always done well. I'll wear this with pride." He touched the VETERAN button on his shirt.

"It's pretty wonderful, isn't it?" Janet agreed. "I hope you get to enjoy the festival, and I hope you'll find Harry today."

"Maybe so." He took the coffee but avoided her gaze.

"Is your last name Milken also?" Janet asked.

"That's right," he said.

"It's nice to meet you, John Milken. I'm Janet Shaw. We're so glad you're here."

"Thank you," he said, but he still wouldn't meet her gaze.

Once he walked out, Janet turned to Debbie, who was wrapping up silverware nearby. "Was that weird?"

"Definitely," her friend confirmed. "I don't know what's going on, but as soon as you mentioned Harry, he got weird."

"Which is odd, because he's the one who asked about Harry in the first place."

"Let's ask Harry about him when he comes in," suggested Debbie.

But Harry didn't come in that morning. Janet wondered if everything was all right. Should she call him? But the morning was busy, and she spent most of her time in the kitchen frying up eggs and pancakes.

She was behind the counter when a young man greeted her from the other side of the register. "Good morning, Mrs. Shaw. Two iced lattes, please."

Janet glanced up and smiled, but it still took her a moment to recognize the man as Ethan Meyers, the newest hire on the police force. Today he wore a polo shirt, khaki shorts, and white sneakers. A pair of reflective sunglasses were tucked into the neck of his shirt.

"Hi, Ethan," Janet said. "I didn't recognize you at first in civilian clothes."

"He would wear his uniform all the time if he could," said the young woman next to him. She was petite, with long dark hair and olive skin, and she wore a coral-color sundress and white strappy sandals. "But every so often I make him take a day off."

"Janet, this is Rachel, my fiancée."

"Congratulations," Janet said as Rachel held up her left hand, revealing a sparkly diamond ring. It had to be at least a carat, and it was surrounded by smaller diamonds as well. "That ring is gorgeous."

"Thank you," Rachel said. "We just got it."

"We've been engaged for a while," Ethan explained. "But today we finally bought a ring."

"That's wonderful," Janet said.

"Well worth waiting for," Debbie chimed in as she walked behind Janet, carrying a tray of scones fresh from the oven.

"Thank you." Rachel slid her arms around Ethan's waist. "We're really excited."

"I should say so." Janet handed them the iced lattes. "In honor of your engagement, these are on the house."

"Oh, you don't have to do that," Rachel protested.

"Congratulations from us." She waved away the twenty-dollar bill Ethan tried to hand her. "Go out and celebrate."

"Thank you, Janet." Ethan smiled and waved goodbye, and Janet watched him and Rachel as they left the café, arm in arm. What a lovely couple. She watched through the window as they walked over to a sports car—a convertible—and climbed in. The car was so new it still had the dealer plates. She would tell Ian about Ethan's engagement tonight when he got home.

"That's unique," Debbie said, scooting the scones off the baking tray and into the display case, the parchment paper crinkling. "Getting engaged but waiting to buy a ring."

"I don't know," Janet said. "I think there are plenty of couples who don't get rings or wait to get them. Maybe they wanted to establish that they were going to get married, but they couldn't afford the ring yet. And things are so expensive these days. Ethan probably wanted to make sure she knew his intentions before he could afford the ring he thought she deserved."

"I suppose you're right. I guess a lot of things are done differently these days." Debbie arranged the last of the scones in the display and carried the empty tray back to the kitchen.

"So true," Janet said, but she kept thinking about the situation after she returned to the kitchen. Ethan's engagement situation wasn't all that unusual. But that was quite a ring he'd given Rachel. And the car he was driving... How had he afforded that on an entry-level police officer's salary? Why had he suddenly been able to afford the ring? Was the timing strange, or was she reading too much into things? She shook her head. Why was she so suspicious? For all she knew, the car was Rachel's.

Patricia arrived. Janet and Debbie chatted with her for a while and then with the couple selling T-shirts at the festival, as well as a pair of workers setting up the tent where festivalgoers would be able to buy traditional fair food, lemonade, and soft drinks.

The lunch rush was in full swing when Todd Mills stepped into the café. The contractor had stopped by several times throughout the process of renovating the Pullman, usually for coffee, though he'd bought other things as well.

"Hello, Todd." Janet struggled to keep her face neutral. Knowing what she knew about him now, she wasn't sure she would be able to keep her dislike from showing. "What can I get you? Are you interested in lunch?"

"Hi, Janet. Actually, I'm not here to eat." Todd had graying brown hair and a mustache, and he was dressed in pressed khakis and a button-down. Every time Janet had seen him, he'd been wearing something similar, and she and Debbie had joked that he was the best-dressed contractor they'd ever met. "I was hoping you could tell me where Kim is."

"I'm afraid I don't know," Janet said. The museum and the Whistle Stop Café were both located in the old train depot, and they worked together on a lot of things, but they were separate. She didn't know Kim's schedule. "She's not at the museum?"

"No. And I really wanted to speak to her today."

"Have you tried her cell phone?"

Todd snapped his gum. "Several times."

"Well, she's in charge of this veterans' homecoming festival, so I imagine she's pretty busy, but I bet she'll call you back when she gets the chance." Or maybe she wouldn't. He might have to talk to her through her lawyer. But that wasn't for Janet to say.

Todd nodded but didn't reply. He also didn't appear ready to leave. Janet had a restaurant full of customers behind him, but she didn't want to be rude. She decided to use the situation as an opportunity.

"Kim took us on a tour of the Pullman," she said. "It turned out beautifully. I love how you managed to preserve so many of the original details. Was it hard to find authentic materials or good reproductions?" She waited to see if he would take the bait.

"That's my specialty," Todd said. "Historically accurate renovations. I know where to find the right materials."

Janet was taken aback by his answer. He spoke so confidently that she almost believed him—until she realized he had answered her vaguely, without addressing the Pullman project specifically. Perhaps that was how he managed to convince so many customers to overlook red flags and trust him. He explained what he was capable of rather than admitting to the poor quality of work he actually delivered.

"It was a beautiful old train car to begin with," Todd continued. "I'm glad we were able to bring it back to life. The first guests are set to check in today."

"That's wonderful." Janet tried a different tactic. "You've done so many impressive historical renovations. Which one was your favorite?"

"Oh, that's a tough one," he said. "I don't think I can choose. Each project is special." He paused. "Although I did get to manage a restoration of one of the biggest houses in Pittsburgh, and that was something else. It was originally built by a steel tycoon, and the new owners spared no expense to bring it back to its original glory. Gilded moldings, coffered ceilings, hand-painted murals—the whole nine yards."

"Wow. I bet that was a big project."

"They all are." He laughed. "I also did a historic inn. That was really fun too."

Janet wondered if he was referring to the Moonlight Historic Inn, one of the projects she knew he'd been sued for.

"I'm working on one now down in Columbus, at the university. It's an old house they're turning into a gallery space. I have another one that's a private home overlooking the lake in Cleveland."

"It sounds like you go all over the place."

"I go where the jobs are, but the local projects are my favorite. That's why I loved working on the Pullman so much. It was a small job for me, honestly, but since my wife grew up here and we live here, I have a soft spot for the history of this place."

Janet was trying to figure out how to work the conversation around to asking where he'd been on Tuesday night, when he suddenly seemed anxious to get going.

"Anyway, if you see Kim, can you tell her I'm looking for her?" he asked.

"I will," Janet promised.

She watched him go, galled. She couldn't believe he got away with the things he did. And she didn't know why he wanted to talk to Kim, but she couldn't imagine Kim would be happy to see him.

CHAPTER TWELVE

More visitors were in town today, and Janet was having fun talking with veterans from all different eras and their families. She met a Vietnam vet, as well as several veterans of the first and second Gulf wars, one from Korea, and even one who'd served in Kosovo.

"Thanks so much for coming out," she said to a man who'd served in Vietnam. He sat with a woman Janet assumed was his daughter, as well as two young adults she thought were likely grandchildren.

"I wouldn't have missed this," he said. "It's so wonderful what you all are doing to make us feel appreciated."

"You are appreciated," Janet insisted. "Veterans should get more recognition for the sacrifices they've made."

"Well, this Reuben sandwich goes a long way," he said with a chuckle.

"Thank you," the daughter said. "This is such a nice thing you all are doing."

Janet smiled. "We're simply doing what we do every day. The person behind the festival is Kim Smith, who runs the depot museum. It's full of fascinating history about this station and this area. Make sure you check it out."

"We certainly will," the woman said.

The café was so busy that they stayed open an hour later than usual. After they'd finally closed and said goodbye to Paulette, Debbie turned to Janet.

"Do you have to go home right away? I was thinking I might check out the festival now since we'll be extra busy tomorrow."

Debbie and Janet planned to set up the deep fryer and make doughnuts outside the café in the morning. They'd already hauled the fryer out of storage and purchased jugs of oil.

"That sounds good." Janet didn't need to rush home for any particular reason, and she was eager to see how Kim's hard work had paid off.

They locked up the café and walked to the festival. The sun beat down, but everyone seemed to be in good spirits.

"That must be the USO movie tent," Debbie said, pointing to a large tent with a white screen against the back wall. They would project the film onto the screen after dark. "Greg and I are going to it tomorrow night."

"That should be fun." It was nice to see Debbie so happy with Greg. Their relationship was still in its early stages, but Janet had a good feeling about it. "What movie?"

"*Casablanca*."

"A classic. Have fun."

Debbie smiled.

"I guess that's where the reenactment is going to be," Janet said, pointing to an open space with bleachers set up along one side.

Crowds of people browsed the stalls and admired the artifacts that Kim had brought out. The scent of grilling meat wafted from the food tent, which would probably become much more crowded now that the café was closed for the day. Veterans in uniform mixed with children and young couples.

"This is pretty great," Debbie said. "Kim did an awesome job putting it together."

"She really did," Janet agreed.

They wandered past a display about the history of the canteen. At the very bottom of the display was a photo of Janet and Debbie posing in front of the café.

There was also a row of booths along the back of the museum, where vendors had set up displays of antique medals and uniforms, custom dog tags, and wooden cutting boards imprinted with the logos of different branches of the military. Next to the cutting boards was the booth of T-shirts and sweatshirts operated by the visitors who'd been in the café several times during the past week.

"Well, hello," the man greeted them. "It's good to see you."

"What a great setup," Janet said, fingering a sweatshirt. The shirts were displayed in neat stacks, and it felt like they were made of high-quality materials. "How's business?"

"We aren't selling too many sweatshirts in this heat," the woman said. "But we've sold a fair number of T-shirts."

Janet eyed an army sweatshirt for their friend Ray Zink, who lived at Good Shepherd Retirement Center, as Debbie said, "You sure have an all-inclusive collection."

The man behind the table beamed. "We've worked really hard to make sure there's something for everyone. We've tried to include every kind of veteran, especially the ones we don't usually see mer-chandise for. We believe everyone deserves to be represented and be proud of serving our country."

"What a great philosophy," Debbie said.

Janet ended up buying the sweatshirt for Ray and, after chatting with the couple a little longer, she and Debbie left the booth.

They continued along and found Carrie Wilson sitting in a booth that said CLOTHING DRIVE FOR VETERANS along the back. The booth was lined with collection bins that were partially filled with clothes.

"Hi, Carrie." Debbie waved. "This seems to be going well so far."

"We already have several bins full," Carrie said. "Austin had to take a load home."

"That's great news," Janet said.

"And here comes someone with more." She smiled as Rick Overton, who went to Faith Community Church, made his way toward them with a full trash bag.

"We'll leave you to it," Janet said, and they continued down the line. Part of her wished she could ask Carrie more questions about the night of the fire, but she doubted they would get anything more than what they already knew. She would love to quiz Austin or Tyler, but they weren't here, and she couldn't think of a way to talk to them that wouldn't interfere with Ian's investigation.

"Check it out." Debbie pointed to the end of the row of booths, where glass display cases on tables showed old guns. "There's our friend Jedidiah Merrick."

"Let's go say hello."

They approached the booth and found Jedidiah seated on a folding plastic chair in the middle of the display. He wore a straw hat to protect his face from the sun along with shorts and a short-sleeved button-down. The grazes were still evident on his cheeks, and his hand was still bandaged.

"Hello," Debbie said. "This is a fantastic display."

"Thank you." Jedidiah ducked his head. "Sorry I didn't make it in today. Your food is still the only good thing about this town."

Janet tried not to show how much his words hurt. This was her hometown. "I'm sorry you're not enjoying it. We love it here."

"What is it that's bothered you?" Debbie asked. "Maybe we can help make it better."

"Not unless you can get that wreck of a police department into shape."

Debbie placed her hand on Janet's arm, letting her know that she meant to handle this. "It sounds like something happened to you in Dennison."

Janet bristled at his words, but she tried not to show it. She kept a sympathetic smile on her face.

He looked from Janet to Debbie and back again, and then he said, "I'm staying out at the campground over by the lake. When I'm on the road, I stay in my RV and pull the trailer with my merchandise. Keeps it safe and makes it easy. I should have known something was wrong with this campground the minute I got there. They lost my reservation. I'd gone on their website and reserved one of the best spots, right next to the lake. Of course, they'd given it away, and the rest of the lake spots were taken by the time I got there, so I had to set up by the bathrooms. Apparently, it was the last place left. I didn't want to hear people coming and going all night, but they said it was that or nothing. Is that any way to treat a customer?"

"I'm sorry," Janet said. "That does sound frustrating."

"It was a Monday night. It wasn't as if the place was full. There were plenty of open spots. But they kept saying those were reserved. What about my reservation?"

"That's really too bad," Debbie said sympathetically. "I'm sorry."

"The people in the next trailer over sat outside drinking and arguing for most of the evening. I sat in my trailer and tried to block it out with music, but they kept banging on the door, telling me to keep it down."

That campground had always seemed idyllic to Janet, but Jedidiah made it sound terrible.

"Anyway, I was in there polishing a few of my best antiques. I like to keep them nice and shiny for the display."

"They are beautiful," Janet said. If someone liked old guns anyway.

"They're pretty, but they also carry great historical significance," Jedidiah said.

Janet wanted to get back to his story. "So, you had some of them in your camper with you?" she prompted.

"That's right," he said. "It was around ten, and I was about to start putting things away and getting ready for bed when I heard someone outside trying to open my trailer."

"You could hear that from inside the RV?" Janet was skeptical about that.

"Clear as day. It was locked, of course, but I heard someone monkeying with the handle. I knew they were trying to get inside. Some of these antiques are incredibly valuable, and I knew someone was trying to steal them. So obviously I went out there. I still had one of the guns in my hand—a Springfield Trapdoor 1873."

He paused as if he expected them to be impressed, and when neither woman replied, he sighed and said, "That's the weapon that was used by the 7th Cavalry at the Battle of the Little Bighorn."

Janet nodded as if she remembered everything from her history classes decades before. She did recall that the battle had been between Indigenous Americans and US troops, and vaguely remembered something about Custer's Last Stand.

"So you took the gun outside with you?" Debbie asked.

"I went out there and found a woman trying to get into my trailer. I shouted for her to get away, and she started shrieking that she'd gotten the wrong trailer and thought mine was hers. She also screamed about how I waved a weapon at her. Now, the Trapdoor is over a century old. If it had been loaded, which it was not, it doesn't even shoot anymore. She didn't really think I threatened her with a loaded weapon. But she'd been caught and had to find something to blame on me."

Janet and Debbie exchanged a glance. Was this a lead?

"Well, soon enough the police show up, and next thing I know, I'm getting arrested for threatening this lady with a dangerous weapon. She didn't get in trouble for trying to steal my stuff, naturally. She turned on the waterworks and sobbed about how she was confused and then I threatened her and she was so scared—" He broke off and shook his head. "It was textbook police incompetence. Unreal."

Again, Janet tried not to show how much the words bothered her. "You were arrested?"

"Handcuffed, fingerprinted, the whole thing. I was finally released sometime in the early morning, but they kept my Trapdoor. How am I supposed to make any money if they take my most valuable merchandise?"

"It sounds like you were treated terribly," Debbie said sympathetically.

Janet understood his frustration. But she also understood that to someone who didn't know the gun was an antique and unloaded, it could have been frightening to see him come charging out of the camper with it.

"You better believe it. Someone's trying to steal my stuff, and I'm the one who gets arrested?" He scowled. "And then the police have the nerve to come over to my trailer last night asking me about a fire at a warehouse I've never heard of. They seemed to think I set it as some kind of revenge plot, because I guess the Trapdoor was inside. That doesn't make any sense. Even if I'd known where they kept the gun, which I didn't, why would I set fire to the place and burn my own property?"

When he put it that way, Janet had to admit that it sure didn't make a whole lot of sense.

"It's a pretty lousy way of telling someone that they not only took your gun unfairly but they also let it burn up in a fire. I'm thinking of suing, to be honest."

"On what grounds?" Debbie asked.

"For gross negligence, and to cover the cost of the gun."

"Your antiques aren't insured?" Janet asked.

"They are, but that's not the point. They can't treat people this way, taking their property and then accusing them of setting fire to a warehouse out of spite. It's not right." He crossed his arms over his chest. "I told them I couldn't have burned down that warehouse, because I was at that pizza place in town—something or other Vita—watching the game all night. I told 'em to go talk to the owner, who saw me there and would vouch for me. I guess they must have done that, because I haven't heard from them since."

"I'm so sorry you've had such a bad experience in Dennison," Debbie said, her voice soothing.

"On top of all of that, they're tracking me. Somehow they knew that I shopped at the army surplus store in New Philadelphia on my way in. They even know what I bought."

"They do?" Janet tried her best to sound oblivious. If he hadn't figured out how the police knew what he'd bought and where, she certainly wasn't going to enlighten him.

"What did you buy that they were so concerned about?" Debbie asked.

He rolled his eyes. "Apparently stuff that was super-suspicious. I bought rope to tie down some of the stuff in the trailer. The old one was worn out. I bought a knife to cut the rope. I got a new pair of gloves because I always use gloves to clean the antiques and my old ones needed to be replaced. The solvent will damage your skin if you don't wear the proper protection."

Janet hadn't considered he might have legitimate reasons for his bizarre shopping list.

"I also got some T-shirts and a glass bottle to hold solvent. I don't like keeping the big jug of it inside my camper, so it's usually out in the trailer, but I like to have a small amount inside for cleaning. Apparently, those things together make me the kind of guy who makes Molotov cocktails. The cops in this town really are unbelievable. I'm thinking of leaving the festival early. I'm starting to feel that the longer I stay, the more I'm opening myself up to their shenanigans."

"It sounds like you've been treated poorly." Janet could understand how it might feel that way to him, especially since he didn't know the local police the way she did. "I'm sorry."

"Did you get those scratches while you were here too?" Debbie asked.

"Sure did. I tripped over a root at the campground on my way back to the camper on Tuesday night. When I went to complain about the roots, the campground owner—the one who lost my reservation—tried to claim I was drunk and that's why I tripped. I'd had a few, but that's not why. I tell you. This place."

"I hope your visit gets better." Janet didn't want to stand there and listen to him demean her town or her husband any longer. "It really is a lovely town."

He grunted, and she and Debbie moved on.

"He sure doesn't like Dennison," Debbie said when they were out of earshot.

"It sounds like he's had a rough time," Janet said.

"You're being very generous, considering the way he talked about the town and the police."

Janet was determined to be generous, even if she didn't want to be around him. "It sounds like he has some valid complaints about the campground, at least. And if that woman tried to break into his trailer, I can see how he feels he was treated unfairly. Especially since he lost his gun to the fire."

"I'm sure the police would have done something about it if he had a legitimate complaint," Debbie said. "The more important question is whether we believe him. He claims he didn't set the fire."

"You know, I think I do," Janet said. "He has an alibi. And he's right that it doesn't make sense for him to have set the warehouse on fire as some sort of revenge. Not when it would destroy the gun he wanted back."

"And his explanation for the items on the receipt sounded legit," Debbie agreed.

"Exactly," said Janet.

"We could go to Buona Vita and ask if he was there on Tuesday night," Debbie said.

"I'm sure the police have already done that," Janet said. "Ian will know whether his alibi checks out. I don't know how much good it would do for us to go too. If it didn't check out, I bet Jedidiah would be in police custody by now."

"Besides, we don't know how he would have gotten into the warehouse," Debbie said. "If it was someone who had access to a key, directly or indirectly, it seems unlikely it was Jedidiah."

"We don't know how any of the suspects would have gotten into the warehouse," Janet pointed out. She didn't say it out loud, but whoever had gotten into the warehouse also had to get into the evidence cage. The most likely scenario was that someone had gotten ahold of the key. But Ian had said that, unlike the warehouse, there were only two existing keys to the cage. Ethan Meyers flashed back to her mind.

"You're right," Debbie said. "That's a problem we have yet to solve."

Janet let out a sigh. "Well, in any case, it sounds like he's probably not our arsonist."

"I think you're right." Debbie nodded at the café. "Do you see that?"

A woman stood outside the café. Her arms were crossed over her chest, and she wore knee-length denim shorts and a black T-shirt. A tall man with a mustache stood next to her, wearing shorts and a shirt with the sleeves ripped off.

"Is that Jennie Ward?" Janet asked.

"I think it is."

"Why is she waiting outside the café?"

"I don't know," Debbie said. "I guess we'd better go find out."

CHAPTER THIRTEEN

Janet could tell the moment Jennie saw them coming. Her shoulders straightened, almost as if she wanted to make herself appear taller.

Janet stopped short, and beside her, Debbie did the same. "Can we help you with something?"

"Stay off my property." Jennie glowered. "If I catch you there again, you'll be sorry."

"Okay," Janet said slowly. "We will?"

Jennie pointed at her. "I came here to tell you to stay away."

"Yeah, we got the message loud and clear," Debbie said. "And we already told you we would."

"That was before I found out *she's* married to a cop." Jennie scowled at Janet.

"We're not working with the police," Debbie told her.

The man with Jennie snorted. "Yeah, right."

"How did you find out who we were, anyway?" Janet asked.

"You told me your names," Jennie said. "I may not be a genius, but even I can remember a couple of names long enough to get to the internet." She jerked a thumb at the café. "It's how I figured out where to find you too, in case you hadn't put that together yet."

"Okay." A hundred questions sprang to Janet's mind, but one took priority. "Why did you come here?"

"Because I don't like people messing with my stuff," Jennie said. "So I wanted to make sure you got the message."

"Message received," Debbie said.

Jennie sized up Debbie then finally spun on her heel and stalked back to the pickup truck she'd driven at their first encounter. The man followed her.

"That was strange," Janet said.

"Coming to the café to threaten us is pretty extreme, considering all we did was drive onto an abandoned property," Debbie agreed.

"Now that I think about it, doesn't it seem a bit strange to have motion-detection cameras guarding a burned-down house?" Janet asked.

"I was so rattled that I didn't think about that yesterday, but now that you mention it, yes," Debbie said. "What are you thinking?"

"Nothing yet. I'm just wondering why. Is there something on the property she doesn't want anyone to find out about?"

"Like what?"

"Like some piece of evidence about the arson that the police haven't yet found?" Janet suggested.

"Or maybe some evidence that connects her to the warehouse fire?" Debbie raised an eyebrow. "It could be anything, really."

"Or maybe it's nothing," Janet said. "Maybe she's just a very private person."

"A private person with something to hide," Debbie said. "Either way, I think we should tell Ian about this."

Janet hesitated. She could see why Debbie thought it was a good idea. It did seem like the kind of thing he should know about.

"Okay," Janet said. "Let's go tell him."

The police station was housed inside Village Hall, a three-story brick building on Grant Street, along with the fire department, city council chambers, and the mayor's office.

Janet and Debbie stepped into the bustling station and approached the front desk, where police receptionist Veronica Burrow, a no-nonsense fiftysomething from Queens, New York, sat smiling at them. Behind her, the open room was filled with half a dozen desks, and behind that, a briefing room with big windows took up half of the back wall. A small holding cell and Ian's office were on the southern wall, across from the kitchen area and the bank of windows that faced the street.

"Hi, Veronica," Janet said. "We're here to see Ian."

"He's in a meeting right now." Veronica smiled at her. "But you're welcome to have a seat and wait."

Janet spotted two other men in Ian's office. She was pretty sure one of them was Walt Kearney, from the Tuscarawas County Sheriff's Department, and she assumed the other man worked with him.

Janet and Debbie perched in the plastic chairs in the waiting area. Brendan was at his desk, working on his computer. All was quiet until Captain Hernandez brought a young man into the station in handcuffs and walked him to the holding cell. Judging by the state of the man and the waves of sour alcohol smell wafting from him, he'd been brought in for public intoxication.

"What about my phone call?" he shouted. "Don't I get a phone call?" His words were slurred.

"You'll be able to contact someone soon." The captain closed the cell door behind the man. "For now, you'll need to hang tight." He walked over to a desk and started typing something on his computer. *No doubt filing the necessary paperwork*, Janet thought.

The man banged on the bars of the cell, demanding his phone call. "This is illegal! You can't hold me here like this! I want to talk to a lawyer! I'll sue all of you!"

Veronica didn't even flinch at the noise. When her desk phone rang, she reached for it calmly. "Dennison Police Department." She listened for a few seconds. "Hold on. I'll get a report started. Where did you say the noise was coming from?"

Janet tried to listen to Veronica handle the complaint, but she was distracted by the noise the drunk man was making. The officers inside the station were apparently unfazed by the ruckus. Less than a minute after Veronica ended the call, she took another one, which appeared to be someone reporting a stolen bicycle. While she took down the information, Brendan stood up, stretched, and said to the captain, "I'm headed back out."

"Good luck," Captain Hernandez said. "Although it's not too bad out there, aside from a few folks who've had too much."

"Summer weekend." Brendan shrugged. "Let's hope the action doesn't pick up."

Veronica answered the phone again. "And where was the RV parked?" she asked a moment later.

"I want to talk to my lawyer!" the man in the holding cell bellowed again. "I'll sue!"

"Down by the creek," Veronica repeated, making a note. "Yeah, I know the place. That big sycamore on the corner? That house has such a nice porch."

"You can't treat me this way. Don't you know who I am?"

"Your dad's car dealership doesn't mean you can ignore the law," Brendan called over his shoulder as he walked toward the door.

"Was the gas tank full the last time you were inside the vehicle?" Veronica asked into the phone.

Brendan passed Veronica's desk. He smiled and waved. "Hi, Janet. Debbie. How are you both doing?"

"Fine, Brendan," Janet said. "And you?"

"As well as can be expected," Brendan replied. "Have a good afternoon. Chief should be out soon." He nodded to Ian's office. "As soon as he's done with the guys from the sheriff's office."

"Thank you," Janet said.

"Is there any chance someone drove it since Sunday?" Veronica asked. Then a moment later she said, "Okay, so it could have happened any time since Sunday?"

Brendan walked out, and Janet waited while Veronica finished her phone call.

"Busy day, huh?" Janet asked, smiling at Veronica after she hung up.

"Not too bad, considering," Veronica said. "We have a lot of officers getting overtime at the festival, but the crowd seems pretty well-behaved, so it's mostly normal weekend stuff." She glanced at the man in the holding cell.

Even "normal weekend stuff" was enough to make Janet very grateful when Ian's visitors finally left and Veronica told her to go on in.

"Hi, Janet. Debbie." Ian smiled up at them from behind his desk. "Sorry to keep you waiting. What brings you in today?"

"Jennie Ward was waiting for us outside the café this afternoon," Janet said.

"She came specifically to warn us to stay away from her property," Debbie added.

"She was at the café?" Ian cocked an eyebrow.

"We walked through the festival, and she was there when we came back," Debbie said. "She'd already told us to stay off her property, and we'd agreed to it, but she felt the need to come and tell us again anyway."

"How did she know where to find you?" Ian asked.

"We gave her our names," Janet said. "When we talked to her yesterday."

"We were trying to be friendly," Debbie added.

Ian sighed, and Janet rushed on. "Remember how I told you that Jennie has motion-activated cameras set up on the property?"

"I do."

"Well, when she showed up today, we thought about that and couldn't help but wonder why they'd bother to set up cameras," Janet said.

"It's a little strange, don't you think?" Debbie said. "Considering the only thing that's supposedly on the property is a burned-out house she set fire to?"

"*Allegedly* set fire to," Ian corrected.

"Allegedly set fire to," Debbie amended.

"But the fact that she was so insistent about keeping us off the property made us think she might have something to hide on the property itself," Janet said. "And we thought you should know about it."

"Do you have any idea what she might be hiding on the property?" Ian asked. Janet couldn't tell if he took them seriously or not.

"I don't," Debbie said. "But given the way she acted, it's not unreasonable to think she's hiding evidence that could tie her to the fire at the warehouse."

"But you didn't see anything of that nature at the Clasp Hollow property?"

"No," Janet admitted.

Ian asked a few follow-up questions about their interactions at the abandoned property yesterday and then at the café today, and then he said, "Thanks for coming in. You did the right thing telling me about this."

"Will you be home for dinner?" Janet asked.

"I'll do my best," Ian said.

They left the station, and Debbie drove through the streets of Dennison, which were crowded now that the festival was in full swing. Janet decided it would be quicker to walk to the café parking lot, so Debbie dropped her off a couple of blocks from the depot.

"See you in the morning!" Debbie called, and Janet waved and started toward the small lot on foot. As she walked, she exchanged greetings with a few people who were out enjoying the late afternoon and the festivities.

She was surprised to run into Todd Mills again. He stood outside the depot museum, watching people stroll up and down the line of booths. By the way he was chomping his gum, Janet could tell he was agitated.

"Hey, Janet."

"Hello, Todd. Enjoying the festival?"

"Sure." But his expression said otherwise.

Janet wasn't sure what to say. If he wasn't enjoying it, why was he still hanging around? She scanned the area, but he didn't seem to be there with anyone.

"Did you ever find Kim?"

"Yes." He didn't offer anything else.

"Good," she said, unsure what else to say. She wanted to know how his conversation with Kim had gone, but he probably wouldn't tell her. And even if he did, she wasn't sure she'd believe his version. "Are you waiting for something?"

"It would be nice if someone would convince her to pay me." She caught a whiff of a strange fragrance coming from him. It was a little spicy, a little sweet. It almost smelled like anise, but different.

"Excuse me?"

"I'm still waiting on my final payment for my work on the Pullman. She refuses to pay it, and I really need the money."

Janet struggled to think of how to respond.

"If you see her, will you tell her I'm not giving up until I get paid?"

She bit her lip. Before all this, she'd always thought Todd was a nice guy, but with the way he was acting now and what she'd learned about him, she was getting a distinctly creepy vibe. She had no interest in helping him get what he wanted.

She also might not get another chance to ask him about the problems with the Pullman and the night of the fire. "Actually, I heard that things were kind of contentious between you and the depot museum. Something about work not being done right, or on time?"

"How do they expect me to do the work when they won't pay me what they owe me?" Todd demanded. "I have to get paid, or I can't buy the supplies I need to finish the project."

Perhaps. But that didn't explain why he had been sued for breach of contract by so many people who had hired him. Janet realized she probably wasn't going to get anywhere with this line of questioning. He would merely continue to insist that he had to be paid.

What she really wanted to know was where he was the night of the fire. "Hey, did you hear about that fire at the warehouse Tuesday night?" She was reaching, but she hoped he was too upset to notice. "I'm sure they'll rebuild, given how many city departments use the building. Is that the kind of thing you would ever work on?"

"I heard about it," he said. "But I've never seen the place. It was a modern building, so it's not my kind of thing."

Before she could think of anything that might get him to talk about where he'd been Tuesday night, he waved and said, "Have a good night."

He walked toward the stage and resumed staring out over the crowd.

When she reached her car and checked over her shoulder, he was still there, his arms crossed over his chest.

Janet was still thinking about Todd when she got home, but she had to focus on the task she'd given herself for the afternoon. She wanted to take the list of things she needed to buy for their upcoming trip and check off as many of them as she could.

She took Laddie out for a quick walk, and then she grabbed her list and headed to the store. She parked in the lot and pushed her cart up and down the aisles. Bug spray? Check. Sunscreen? Check. She could use some new shorts, and Tiffany had mentioned something similar. They were on sale, so that helped. She tossed in a couple pairs for herself and some for Tiffany. She also picked up the water shoes Tiffany had requested, as well as flip-flops for herself and shorts and T-shirts for Ian. She grabbed a new cooler and travel toiletries.

She saw that Tiffany had added a few more things to the list, including organic spinach and frozen fruit and several kinds of snacks Janet had never heard of before. It was too soon to buy spinach, which would wilt before the trip. She hadn't realized Tiffany liked spinach that much. She should ask her daughter if she wanted the frozen fruit for smoothies so she would know whether they would need a blender at the cabin.

And the specific snacks Tiffany had asked for—potato chips, gourmet popcorn, kombucha—were brands that Janet had never bought in the past. She wasn't even sure what kombucha was. She asked an employee, who told her it was a drink and helped her find a bottle in the refrigerated section. Janet held it up and read that it was a fermented tea that was supposed to be a good probiotic. She set it into her cart. Tiffany must have tried these things at college.

She pushed her cart to the registers, reflecting on how things had changed. Tiffany was becoming an adult. It made sense that her tastes would evolve, as Janet's had in her own early adulthood. She wondered if her parents had felt the same combination of excitement for her next phase of life and sadness that her childhood years were over.

Janet tried to smile as the woman behind the checkout counter totaled up her purchases. It was much more than she had expected, but the healthier brands did tend to cost more. It would all be worth it when she was sitting on the dock with an ice-cold lemonade in one hand and a book in the other, her feet dangling in the water, and her daughter beside her, drinking her expensive fermented tea.

She got home as Ian pulled into the driveway. She greeted him with a kiss, and he helped her carry the bags in. While she sorted through the purchases and put them in the right rooms, he heated up the grill.

"Will Tiffany be eating with us?" he asked as he set the pork chops on a plate.

"Let me check." Tiffany wasn't home, but she might have texted. Janet pulled out her phone and checked, and sure enough, there was a message from Tiffany.

Hanging out with Hudson and Violet tonight. I won't be out too late.

"No," Janet said. "She's with Hudson and Violet."

"She's been hanging out with Hudson a lot this summer, hasn't she?" Ian asked.

"I guess?" Janet wasn't sure how to judge that. Tiffany had gone to school with Hudson since elementary school, and he was a nice kid. Well, a nice young adult now. Was there something more than friendship between them? "She says she won't be out late," she added, and that seemed to soothe Ian's concerns somewhat.

They sat down at the picnic table, and the golden summer evening felt light and cool against her skin. The tree in the backyard shaded the small deck, and the citronella candles and fairy lights Tiffany had hung from the tree's branches gave the area a soft glow.

"Did you have any luck with the warehouse fire today?" Janet asked.

"Nothing I can tell you about," Ian said.

That wasn't the same as a no. But it wasn't a yes either.

"I'm glad you told me about Jennie," Ian said, cutting a bite from his pork chop. "If she approaches you again, you'll let me know, right?"

"I promise," Janet said. "Did you go out to her property and see if she was hiding something there?"

"We can't show up on private property and snoop around," Ian said. "It doesn't work like that. We need a warrant, and for that, we have to show a judge that we have probable cause."

"And do you?"

"Not yet."

"What would qualify as probable cause?"

Ian raised an eyebrow at her. "Something more than a suspicion that she's hiding something out there."

Janet briefly wondered if she and Debbie should poke around, but dismissed the idea almost immediately. Jennie had made it clear she didn't want them there, and Ian wouldn't want them to do that.

"Well, I hope you find something, and I hope it leads to an arrest in the warehouse fire."

"If she's the one who did it," Ian said. "It doesn't do us any good to arrest the wrong person."

"But surely she's a solid lead," Janet said. "Since she's an arsonist and all."

Janet still had her doubts about Tyler Wilson and possibly his father. And then there was Todd Mills, but Jennie was still a strong suspect.

"An *alleged* arsonist," Ian corrected her. "And I can't talk to you any further about who our current suspects are."

"Okay," Janet said. She ate a few bites of her pork chop and the salad she'd made, and her mind drifted back to her recent interactions with Todd.

"What about Todd Mills?" she asked.

"What about him?"

"I assume you're investigating him as well?"

"We're looking at all possible suspects."

"But you don't think it's him," Janet said. She could tell by the way he'd said it.

"He's involved in a civil dispute," Ian said. "A lawsuit over a few thousand dollars doesn't seem like the kind of crime that would drive someone to set fire to a warehouse."

"I guess so." She couldn't argue with that. And yet, because it was Kim and the depot museum, it felt a lot more personal than the other crimes that had evidence in the warehouse.

Janet decided to try another approach. After all, he'd only said he couldn't discuss suspects with her. "Have you had any luck coming up with how someone might have gotten into the evidence cage? How someone might have been able to get the key?"

Ian set his bite of salad down and peered at her. "Why?"

"I was just wondering."

"Janet, I know you pretty well by now. I know you don't 'just wonder' anything without a good reason. What's going on?"

She supposed that after twenty years of marriage, she should have expected that. She'd better come clean. "I saw Ethan Meyers today. He came into the café with his fiancée."

"His fiancée? I didn't even know he had a girlfriend."

Janet wasn't particularly surprised. Ian cared very much for the people on his squad, but he wasn't known for spending a lot of time discussing their personal lives.

"Apparently, they've been engaged for a while. But he didn't give her a ring until recently. He said he was finally able to afford one."

"That's nice. He must have been saving his paychecks. I'll have to congratulate him."

"It was a nice ring. Big diamond."

"How wonderful." Was there an edge to his voice?

"I also noticed he was driving a sports car. A convertible. It was too new to have real plates yet, so I assume that's a recent purchase as well."

"What are you implying, Janet?" There was a definite edge in his voice now.

"I'm not necessarily implying anything. I simply noticed that he seems to suddenly have come into a fair amount of money."

"As in he may have gotten a payout of some kind?"

"You did say that only people on the squad had access to the key to open the evidence cage," Janet reminded him.

"It couldn't have been Ethan, Janet."

"Why not? It must have been somebody, right?"

"No one on my squad would do something like that," Ian said flatly. "It isn't possible."

"But if that's how the arsonist got in—" Janet began.

"No one on my squad would do something like that," Ian repeated, and there was a finality in his voice. "Besides, you don't know his circumstances, and neither do I. His family could have money, or he may have come into money in another legitimate way. He had nothing to do with setting the fire."

Ian was loyal to his team. That was one thing she loved about him. He always saw the best in everyone he cared about, no matter what. But was that working against him now? In this case, was he refusing to see what was right in front of him?

CHAPTER FOURTEEN

I t was going to be a hot day. Janet could tell from the moment she climbed out of bed on Saturday morning. It was already warm, and the sun wasn't even up yet.

It was going to be a busy day as well. Today was the big field hospital reenactment at the homecoming festival. Janet and Debbie were going to run a doughnut station, like the original volunteers who had given doughnuts to servicemen passing through the depot on their way to war. The big ceremony to honor the vets wasn't until tomorrow, but there was plenty scheduled for today.

But first, coffee. She made a pot and prayed while she got ready. Then she drove through the empty streets to the café. She loved summer mornings, when the night's cooler temperatures had wrung much of the humidity out of the air. She got to work baking at the café, and, as she'd expected, the day was bustling from the moment they flipped the sign to Open.

In addition to their regulars, there was a steady stream of new faces. Janet chatted with veterans, their family members, and even the first family to stay in the Pullman, a man in his fifties and his wife, along with their two teenage children. They were from St. Louis and had come to Dennison specifically to stay in the newly reno-vated train car.

"How is it?" Janet asked when they'd told her where they were staying.

"Fabulous," the man said.

"Small," his son said at the same time.

"It's cozy," the wife clarified. "And that's because it's original."

"The part that pulls down to make a bed is pretty cool," the daughter said.

"Brian is a huge train enthusiast," the woman explained, indicating her husband. "So when we heard about it, we knew we had to try it out."

"Some families go to theme parks," the son said, shaking his head.

His father grinned. "What history can you learn at a theme park?"

"I think it's wonderful, and I'm glad you're all having a good time," Janet said.

Tiffany showed up shortly before they opened, and a few minutes later, Charla Whipple—Janet's former boss at the Third Street Bakery—also came in to help with the doughnuts. Tiffany had taken the day off from the pool. She wore a forties-style dress, her hair up in a period-appropriate twist, and Charla wore a fascinator and a shirt-waist dress that was belted around the waist.

Debbie and Charla moved the doughnut fryer outside and started heating the oil. Janet and Tiffany followed with the table. They set it up then draped a banner that read THE SALVATION ARMY CANTEEN, FREE SERVICE TO SERVICE PERSONNEL across the front. It was a reproduction of the sign that had decorated the table during World War II.

"Why does the banner say the doughnuts are free if you're charging for them?" Tiffany asked as she helped Janet set up the cashbox and credit card payment device. A line was already forming beside the table.

"It's historically accurate," Janet said. "And we *are* giving doughnuts to active-duty service personnel and veterans."

Tiffany grinned. "The help gets free samples, right? For quality assurance?"

Janet chuckled. "Of course."

When Charla started dropping fresh dough into the hot oil, the delicious smell drew an even longer line. Janet and Debbie went back inside when they were confident that Charla and Tiffany could handle things.

Soon afterward, Harry and Crosby came in.

"Hello, Harry," Janet said, ushering him to the counter. "We missed you yesterday. Is everything okay?"

"I was feeling a little under the weather," he said. "But I'm doing better now."

"I'm glad to hear it," Janet said. She took his order and went behind the counter to pour his coffee. "Did your friend ever find you?"

"No, I haven't run into him yet," Harry said, settling down on a stool with Crosby at his feet.

"Maybe today," Janet said. "He was in here yesterday, and I got his last name. He's John Milken."

"Milken?" Harry echoed with a frown.

"I think that was it." Did he recognize the name? She studied his face and realized what she was seeing there. He was familiar with the name but not in a happy way. "You know him."

"I do indeed." Harry didn't elaborate, but his lips were pressed into a thin line.

"If he comes in today looking for you, should I help him find you?" Janet asked, unsure.

Harry didn't answer for a moment. The line behind him grew, but Janet didn't care. She couldn't rush her friend when this obviously pained him somehow.

"Do you know what he wants?" Harry asked at last.

"I don't," Janet said. "I'm sorry."

"I see." Harry lifted his chin. "Crosby and I will be at the festival today. If John Milken comes in again, you can tell him to come find me there."

"I will," Janet said. She gave him his order. "I hope you have a good day."

Janet puzzled over the interaction as she went to the kitchen and fried eggs and flipped pancakes. Later, when she went out to the dining area to see how things were going, she spotted Harry and Crosby sitting on their favorite bench on the train platform, but she didn't see John Milken.

Paulette came in as the lunch rush hit, and Janet didn't have a moment to catch her breath until it was time to close. Once they'd cleaned the café, Paulette went home and Janet and Debbie went out to help with the doughnuts.

They worked the rest of the afternoon, catching glimpses of the reenactment and the forties-era brass band that played World War II favorites. Janet spotted John Milken wandering around but not Harry and Crosby. She wasn't sure if she should hope they connected or not, given Harry's reaction that morning.

Many familiar faces came for doughnuts, and several of Tiffany's friends swung by to see her as well, including Layla, Violet, and Hudson.

By late afternoon, they'd sold out completely, so they cleaned up and packed away the fryer. At Janet's insistence, Charla and Tiffany left Janet and Debbie to finish things up. It had been a successful afternoon. They'd sold hundreds of doughnuts and given away nearly as many.

As they finished, Greg Connor came by the table, wearing a button-down shirt, his hair brushed back.

"Hello, Greg," Janet said, smiling at Debbie's boyfriend.

"Hi. Did you all have a successful afternoon?"

"We did," Debbie said. "And I'm about ready to go."

"You guys are headed to the movie?" Janet asked.

"We're going to get some dinner first," Greg said. "But then, yes."

"*Casablanca* is such a great movie," Debbie said. "It'll be fun to see it like this."

"Then get going. I've got this." Janet shooed them away and watched them go with a smile. She was overjoyed for Debbie. The early days of a relationship were wonderful, though Janet was even happier in the loving relationship she and Ian had built over the past twenty-plus years. Debbie and Greg would get there too.

Janet locked up and was walking to her car to head home when she saw Austin Wilson on the stage, making an announcement about the clothing collection. She wandered over in time to hear him ask people to leave their donations at the table he'd set up near the vendor booths. When he was done, the audience clapped. Then Kim stood and revealed the lineup of activities for the evening, as well as information about the following day's schedule. The festival would end on Sunday afternoon with the ceremony formally recognizing and thanking all veterans.

Janet listened to the announcements and then decided to swing by the clothing donation booth to see if Austin was there. She found him sitting alone in the booth, surrounded by overflowing bins.

"Obviously this has been a success," Janet said, gesturing at the bins. "Congratulations."

"I wish I could do more," he said. "Someday I'd love to set up housing for veterans who need help, but this is what I can do for now."

"What a great idea. How did you come up with it?"

"I've been lucky. I had a great family and a home to return to after my time in Afghanistan. But not all my buddies were so fortunate. What you see over there—it's so hard to adjust to civilian life afterward. And many of them had injuries, both the kind you can see and the kind you can't. I want everyone who serves this country to have the help they need to get back on their feet. After what they sacrifice, they should never have to worry about things like food and housing again."

Listening to him, Janet felt bad for even considering him a suspect. How could such a man have burned down a warehouse? She almost didn't ask what she'd come to ask him. But if she got it over with, she could cross him off her list entirely. So before she could change her mind, she asked, "How's Tyler doing? I hope that fire at the warehouse didn't affect him."

"Why would it affect him?" A moment before, Austin had seemed so open, but there was something guarded in the way he answered her. Did he really not know how the fire could have an impact on Tyler's case, or was he hiding something?

"Isn't his trial coming up soon?" She tried to sound as nonchalant as possible. "I heard the part of the warehouse that burned was related to police matters."

He raised his eyebrows as if this was new information for him, but Janet's internal lie detector went off. He knew this, she was certain. "I hope it won't delay Tyler's trial. We want to put this all behind us so we can move forward."

"I hope so too," she said. "A trial is a big ordeal. I would want it over with as well." She was quiet for a moment, pretending to consider an idea. "Has he ever thought about pleading guilty to avoid the hassle of a trial?"

"Why would he do that?" Austin seemed affronted by the idea. "Sure, he might have had a drink or two, but they don't know if he was over the legal limit or not. Having a guilty plea on his record would be a big red flag for colleges. It would ruin his future."

At first, she suspected that Austin was in denial in the same way his wife had been, refusing to acknowledge the possibility that Tyler might have driven under the influence. But after reflecting for a moment, Janet realized that wasn't what Austin had said. He said there was no *proof* Tyler had driven under the influence, not that he hadn't. It was a subtle distinction, but an important one, especially when all the evidence the police had—the evidence that would have made a strong case against Tyler, even in the absence of a breath test—had been destroyed in the warehouse fire.

"I suppose in that case, it works out for Tyler that the police evidence is gone."

He narrowed his eyes. Had she overstepped? "I wouldn't say it's a good thing that the police warehouse burned," Austin said. "That's a terrible thing. Who knows what actual criminals might go free because of it?"

"It is a terrible thing," she agreed quickly. He had managed to twist that around on her, and she wanted to get back in charge of the conversation. "I know Ian is working hard to figure out what happened."

Austin nodded. "He came by and talked to Tyler. Asked questions about his sponsorship with Crackerjack Bats and what kind of gum he chews and all sorts of strange things. I know they think he's a suspect. But Tyler was at a movie that night. The police already talked to his cousin Rex, who drove him, and to the manager at the theater, who vouched for him. He saw Tyler going in before the movie and coming out afterward. Tyler didn't set that fire, if that's what you're hinting at."

"I'm not trying to suggest anything," Janet insisted. "I know the police are digging into this. I just hope they find out who did it."

Austin took in a few deep breaths and then let them out slowly. "I'm sorry if I came across as harsh," he said. "It's hard to see people suspecting Tyler of this on top of the crash. You're a parent. You know how it is to want to protect your child."

"I know exactly how that is." Janet didn't need to be reminded of how often she wanted to hem Tiffany in and keep her from making bad choices. She had to fight against the urge every day to protect her from the dangers of the world, even now that she was mostly grown up.

"I want him to have a fair shot, you know?" Austin said. "Not to let one bad decision ruin the rest of his life."

And there it was. Austin didn't come out and say that he knew Tyler had driven under the influence, but he implied it. He didn't want that bad decision to ruin Tyler's chances. It was a good motivation, a powerful one that any parent would understand. The question was, what lengths would Austin go to in order to protect his son?

"Besides," he went on, "Tyler didn't have a way to get into the evidence cage. How would he have gotten inside to start the fire?"

"I don't know if they've figured out how the person got in," she said. "But I know they're chasing that too."

There was a beat of silence, and Janet's mind caught on something he had said. But before she could ask him about it, Austin said, "Looks like someone has another load coming." Librarian Ellie Cartwright carried a full garbage bag toward them. "It was great talking with you, Janet."

She tried to figure out how to stall so she could ask him about what he'd said, but he turned away from her and started chatting with Ellie, and she knew she'd lost her chance.

Janet wandered off, mulling over the exchange. Austin had said the police had followed up on Tyler's alibi, and it checked out. She didn't know if that was true or not. But even if Tyler was in the clear, she didn't know about Austin. Carrie had said he was working Tuesday night. Had Ian verified that? Something about the way he'd spoken about protecting Tyler and making sure one mistake didn't ruin his future—well, it made her think there was more to the story than simple fatherly love.

After all, Austin presumably had access to the Crackerjack bats inside the Wilson home. When Carrie had bought the Black Jack gum at the café, she'd said it was for Tyler, but that didn't mean that

Austin couldn't have had a piece. That he couldn't have accidentally dropped the wrapper at the scene of the crime.

And how had he known about the evidence cage being opened? Hadn't Ian said that detail wasn't public knowledge? Yet somehow Austin had known that was where the fire had started.

She had the unsettled feeling that Austin knew a lot more about the warehouse fire than he'd let on.

CHAPTER FIFTEEN

Ian called to say he would be working late that night and told her not to hold dinner, but he wouldn't tell her what was going on. She hoped that whatever it was, it would bring him closer to solving the case.

Tiffany had showered and changed from her forties-style dress into a pretty, modern sundress.

"Going out?" Janet asked.

"Yep. Layla and Hudson and I are going to the new superhero movie."

"I hear it's long."

"It's supposed to be good though."

"You should probably take a sweatshirt. They always keep those theaters really cool."

"Good point." Tiffany grabbed a sweatshirt off the hook by the door, and then her purse and keys.

"Speaking of Layla and Hudson, do you know anything more about the weekend at the cabin?" Janet asked. "Like where it is, and who's going for sure?"

Tiffany froze. "Actually, I'm not sure about the cabin weekend after all."

"You're not?" Janet's mom radar went up. Something was going on with Tiffany. It didn't seem to be an issue with her friends. Was it some of the other people who would be at the cabin?

"No. I'm just—I don't know. It doesn't sound like that much fun anymore."

"I see." Janet could tell that her daughter wasn't giving her the whole truth. "You sure? It sounded fun before."

"Yeah, I've been thinking about it, and I don't know." She slung her purse over her shoulder. "But I'll keep you posted on what I decide."

"Okay." Janet watched Tiffany walk toward the door. "I'm here, if there's anything you want to talk about."

"I know, Mom," Tiffany said. "Thanks."

Janet watched her go out the door, feeling unsettled. She and Tiffany had always had a close relationship. Tiffany would open up to her when she was ready. But something was off with her, and Janet wished Tiffany would tell her so she could help.

She wasn't sure how much to push, but she knew she had to leave the ball in Tiffany's court. Tiffany was old enough to let her know if she needed her help. It was a big difference from just less than a year ago, when Tiffany had come to her with everything. Their dynamic was changing now that Tiffany was an adult, and Janet was struggling to figure out how to navigate the new landscape.

She sighed. She might as well use the time for vacation prep. She would start gathering the things she knew they would need. She found the beach chairs hanging on hooks in the garage. She pulled them out and opened them up to make sure they weren't damaged. They were all in good shape. She folded them and stacked them next to the brand-new cooler she'd gotten out of her trunk.

Their bikes were lined up against the wall, as usual. She checked them over and found that Tiffany's had a flat tire. She dug out the pump and added air, but it deflated again. They would need a new tire.

Would Tiffany even want to take her bike? They used to love riding on the old railroad trail to the ice cream place a couple of miles away from the cabin. Was that the kind of thing Tiffany would want to do these days? It seemed like so many of her tastes had changed that Janet couldn't be sure. She would ask tomorrow.

For now, she added replacing the bike tire to one of her lists then decided to relax for the rest of the evening. She sat down in front of the television, but she couldn't get her mind to settle. She kept thinking of things to add to her lists, and when she eventually dragged her thoughts away from that, they jumped to Jennie Ward, Todd Mills, and Tyler and Austin Wilson.

Finally, she gave up and went to bed.

She slept fitfully, but since she could sleep in on Sundays, she stayed in bed until after seven a.m.—a gloriously late start for her. Ian had come home at some point, and she crept out of bed quietly to let him sleep. Downstairs, she found Tiffany's keys on the table and her bag on the hook by the door. She'd made it home safely too.

Janet started the coffee, and as she drank it, she spent some time reading the Bible. Her attention caught on James 1:17. *Every good and perfect gift is from above, coming down from the Father of the heavenly lights, who does not change like shifting shadows.*

It was comforting to be reminded that God was the same, yesterday, today, and forever. It felt like everything was changing all around her, but God was steady. He was unchanging. He would lead her through this unsettled time. And Tiffany—the best of all good and perfect gifts—was His. He would lead and guide her, even if her mom didn't always know what to do.

Refreshed, Janet put the Bible away and started to think about what to make for breakfast. Tiffany eventually came downstairs, eyes bleary, and poured herself a cup of coffee.

"You used to tell me coffee was terrible for me," Janet said.

"That was before I experienced the brutal combination of dorms, early morning classes, and midterms," Tiffany said, smiling.

"What do you want for breakfast?" Janet asked.

"How about waffles with strawberries and whipped cream?"

Janet laughed. That had always been Tiffany's request when she was young. She was an adult now, but maybe that didn't mean everything about her was different from when she was a child.

"If you help me make them," Janet said.

Tiffany sliced strawberries and warmed the maple syrup while Janet tackled the waffles, and by the time Ian came downstairs, breakfast was on the table. As they dug in, Janet reminded herself to treasure these moments when their little family was together. Such times would grow fewer and further between as the years went on.

At church Janet and Ian settled into their regular pew while Tiffany went off to sit with her friends. As the first hymn began, Janet looked around. It felt good to see so many members of their church family here. There was Patricia Franklin, Jim Watson, and

Kim and Barry Smith. Debbie and Greg were in the pew behind her and Ian. And there was Carrie with Austin, and—that was Tyler sitting next to Austin. How wonderful. Tyler hadn't been to church in a long time. It was good to see him. His hair was longer and shaggier than before, and he appeared uncomfortable in the pressed shirt that was a size too small for him. But he was here, and Janet was delighted.

Pastor Nick Winston was preaching through the Beatitudes, and today he talked about Matthew 5:7. *Blessed are the merciful, for they will be shown mercy.* Ian slipped out during the final hymn, headed back to the station. She hated that he had to work on a Sunday, but his hours had never been predictable, especially when a huge case like the warehouse fire loomed over him. Janet and Debbie planned to attend the ceremony honoring veterans at the homecoming festival this afternoon anyway.

After the service, Janet chatted with Kim and Pastor Nick's wife, Brenda, before joining Debbie to leave the sanctuary.

"Did you see who was here?" Debbie asked quietly. She wore a linen shift dress and sandals, cool and put together even on this hot day.

"Tyler Wilson? I did notice him," Janet said. "It's good to see him here."

She waved at Carrie and the others, and then Debbie stopped in front of Tyler. "Good morning, Tyler." She held out her hand. "You probably don't remember me. I'm Debbie Albright."

"Hey." He ducked his head as he shook her hand with his free hand. He held a disposable cup of coffee in the other.

Janet stepped up beside Debbie. "Hi, Tyler. It's good to see you again."

"Hi, Mrs. Shaw. How are you?"

"I'm doing all right. It's good to see you at church," Janet said.

"It's nice to be here." He tugged at the cuff of his sleeve.

"We stopped by to see your mom this week," Debbie said. "It was so nice to catch up with her."

"Yeah, she told me," Tyler said. "Thanks for the cookies."

"It's no problem," Janet said. "Have you been to the festival at all? Your parents have been collecting so many clothes for veterans. It's impressive."

"Yeah, it means a lot to my dad," Tyler said. "He's always had a thing for helping other veterans. I think it's great."

"Especially given how much else he has going on."

"Yeah, he's a good guy." Tyler scratched his arm. "He had to take the whole week off last week to get things ready."

"That's a big commitment," Janet said. "He took the whole week off?"

"Yeah. He spent a lot of time making signs and figuring out how to run the clothing drive—you know, how to collect stuff, the best way to get it to the veterans, stuff like that. It was a lot. I guess he had a bunch of vacation saved up that he had to use anyway though."

"That's so commendable of him," Janet said, even as her mind spun. Was Tyler mistaken? Why hadn't Carrie told them that he'd taken the week off?

She didn't realize she'd allowed an awkward silence to fall until Debbie asked Tyler, "So, what have you been up to?"

"Mostly training, physical therapy, trying to get back into shape after I tore my ACL. I'm hoping I can transfer to a school closer to home," Tyler said.

"That's wonderful. I'm sure it must be a lot of work, getting back into shape," Janet said. "That's practically a full-time job, isn't it?"

"It takes up a lot of my time." Tyler shifted his weight from one foot to the other then glanced over at Carrie, who was still chatting away. "I lost my scholarship when I got injured, so I'm really focusing on my future right now."

Carrie said goodbye to her friends and faced Janet and Debbie. "Hello," she said with such exaggerated enthusiasm that Janet suspected she was trying to pull their attention away from Tyler. "It's good to see you both."

"It's great to see you too," Janet said, trying to match her enthusiasm. "How are things?"

The women made small talk for a few minutes while Tyler remained silent. Finally, Carrie said goodbye, slipped her arm through her son's, and steered him away. Austin waited for them by the door and waved to Janet and Debbie.

"Did you catch that?" Janet said as the family walked out.

"About Austin not being at work on Tuesday?" Debbie said. "You bet I did."

"I'm sure Ian has checked out his alibi," Janet said. "As well as Tyler's."

"I'm sure he has too," Debbie agreed. "And he'll know if one of them isn't telling the truth."

Janet still felt unsettled about the situation, but she wasn't sure what to do about it. She couldn't exactly go down to the hospital and demand to know whether Austin had shown up at work Tuesday or not. Ian hadn't liked that they'd gone to the theater, so he would not be pleased if she showed up at the hospital. Besides, it wasn't as if the hospital would violate its employees' privacy by sharing their schedules with the public. "We'll leave it to him to investigate."

"Are you ready to go then?" Debbie indicated the clock on the wall. "The ceremony is in twenty minutes."

"Sure thing." Janet found Tiffany with Hudson and let her know she was leaving.

"Okay, Mom. I have to go in to work soon anyway. I'll call you if I end up having plans after my shift," Tiffany replied.

"Thanks, honey. See you later."

They drove the short distance to the depot and parked. A large crowd was gathered in front of the stage that had been set up beside the depot museum. For much of the weekend, in between announcements, forties-era music had played from the stage, but now a microphone was set up in front of a simple background that said THANK YOU FOR YOUR SERVICE. It was a hot day—hotter than the day before and also more humid, with great roiling clouds building on the horizon. Maybe a thunderstorm would roll in and cool things off. Janet hoped it would wait until after the ceremony.

Many people in attendance wore military uniforms from throughout the decades. Janet spotted Ray Zink in his wheelchair, wearing a hat that said WORLD WAR II. Several men in their late sixties and early seventies wore the olive-green fatigues that showed they'd served in Vietnam, and there were plenty of people, including Austin Wilson, in the light-colored camo that indicated service in the Middle East. He must have made a quick change after church.

"There's the guy who wanted to find Harry." Debbie nodded toward the front of the crowd, where John Milken stood.

"I wonder what the deal is with that," Janet said. "Harry didn't seem pleased to hear his name." She filled Debbie in on what had happened at the café the day before.

Debbie scanned the crowd. "Is Harry here?"

"I don't see him," Janet said.

"You don't think Harry is avoiding this so he doesn't run into John, do you?"

"I have no idea." Janet shrugged. "Harry isn't a veteran, so maybe he's not that interested in the ceremony." Though that seemed unlikely. Janet had met few people more public minded than Harry. He got involved with everything in the community.

"It's also really hot," Debbie said. "And some of these guys are old enough that they shouldn't be out here for long. I hope they get started soon."

"It's hot enough that I don't want to be out here long either," Janet agreed. The heat settled over them like a blanket. She pulled her shirt away from her sticky skin, trying to get air inside to cool her down. She continued to study the crowd, smiling at several neighbors and friends. She wondered if Todd was in the crowd.

"Maybe we should have done doughnuts today after all," Debbie mused. "We'd have made a killing."

"Would you want to be standing over the fryer on a day like this?"

Debbie shuddered. "No thank you. I'm pretty sure that's why the Lord created the Sabbath, now that you mention it."

Janet laughed. "To keep you from having to make doughnuts in the heat?"

"Okay, that might not have been the reason, but I am grateful that we're not open on Sundays."

Finally, Kim walked onto the stage. "Welcome, everyone. I'd like to extend an especially warm welcome to the men and women who have served our country in unform."

A cheer went up from the crowd.

"The American Soldiers Homecoming Tribute Festival has been a wonderful opportunity to honor our veterans and to explore the rich history of the Dennison Railroad Depot and its special place in our nation's history."

Kim launched into the story of how volunteers at the depot had offered hot meals to service personnel on their way to war, which showed that serving the members of the military had always been at the heart of what the depot represented. She recognized the veterans in the crowd, and as she mentioned each engagement and each branch of the military, a cheer went up.

Janet clapped along with everyone else, but she'd noticed someone interesting in the crowd.

Ethan Meyers patrolled the scene alongside Deputy Brendan Vaughn. It made sense that police officers were in attendance. Whenever a large crowd or event was in town, Ian liked to have officers on-site.

But seeing Ethan now, Janet remembered what she'd observed when he came into the café. Ian had said that there was no sign of forced entry into the warehouse, but he didn't want to consider the possibility that one of his officers—the only ones who would have had access to the key—could have opened the door. Ethan had obviously come into a lot of money recently. She might have believed that it hadn't been sudden except that his fiancée had said they just bought the ring and his car was so new it still had the dealership plates. That meant he must have gotten it recently.

Could he have been behind the break-in after all? Janet kept an eye on Ethan throughout the ceremony. There was nothing suspicious about his behavior, but she couldn't get over the idea that he must know more than he was saying.

At the conclusion of the ceremony, Kim brought the band back to the stage to play the national anthem while the audience faced the flag that hung beside the stage.

When Janet looked over, Debbie was wiping tears from her eyes. "Now she's gone and ruined my mascara," Debbie said with a chuckle.

"It was a beautiful ceremony," Janet said. "And a nice end to the festival."

Ethan and Brendan stood by the stage, carefully observing the crowd.

"What is it?" Debbie asked.

"What do you mean?"

"You're eyeing someone."

"I'm not eyeing anyone."

"It's Ethan Meyers, isn't it?" Debbie had noticed the officers too.

Janet sighed. "I can't help thinking about how odd it is that he suddenly came into a lot of money like that."

"Why don't you go talk to him?" Debbie suggested.

"I don't know how Ian would feel about me interrogating one of his officers."

"Well then, don't interrogate him. Go have a conversation. Ian can't be upset if you have a conversation with one of his fellow officers." Debbie pulled her hair back into a ponytail as she spoke. "I mean, if you come right out and ask him if he took a payoff to steal the key so someone could light the evidence warehouse on fire, then Ian would probably be upset. But you won't do that."

"Fair enough," Janet said. "I'll simply congratulate him again on his engagement and say how glad I am to see him and see how it goes from there." Ian always tried to make the squad feel like a family, and normally she wouldn't hesitate to talk to one of his officers if she saw them around town.

"I've been meaning to ask Brendan about his mother anyway," Debbie said.

The two women made their way through the crowd to the two officers.

"Hello, Brendan," Debbie said, smiling.

"Hi, Debbie. Janet." Brendan nodded at them.

"How is your mother doing?" Debbie asked. "I heard she got remarried this spring."

"That's right," Brendan said. "Her new husband is a good guy. We're all really happy she's finally found someone after losing Dad."

"I'm so glad. She deserves to be happy."

"I totally agree," Brendan said.

Janet took advantage of the break in the conversation to address Ethan. "You seem to be always on the clock these days. Is Ian working you too hard?"

"Nah." Ethan laughed. "I need to take time off next week to go to a family thing, so I had to work a lot this week to get my hours in."

"What family thing?" Janet asked.

"We're getting together to commemorate my grandfather," Ethan said. "He passed away a few months ago, and everyone was really emotional at his funeral, understandably. We loved him very much. But since then, we've realized he would have wanted us to get together and remember him in a positive way, so we're doing that as a family next week. There's talk of making it a family tradition."

"That sounds like a nice custom," Janet said.

He smiled. "We think so too. My grandparents lived in Westport, Connecticut, so I had to ask for several days off. It was kind of Chief Shaw to let me take so much time when I haven't been here very long."

"I'm sure he was happy to do it," Janet said. "Family events are important."

"Yeah, they are. And with how generous Pops was to me, it seems especially important to be there, you know?"

"How generous he was?" Most people didn't come out and talk about money, and Janet wasn't sure if she understood.

"Yeah, he was great at saving. We had no idea how much he had until the will was read."

"Your grandfather left you money?" Debbie said. "How nice."

"I mean, he split it between me and my brothers, naturally, but it was still enough that I was able to buy that ring for Rachel. And now we'll be able to put a down payment on a house, which is great."

"Don't forget that new car," Brendan said. "That's a sweet ride."

"I mean, I'm not going to argue about that," Ethan said, laughing. "But Pops literally had it in his will that he wanted us to make one big frivolous purchase apiece. Normally, I would have found a used vehicle in good shape or something."

"You were able to buy those things because of an inheritance from your grandfather?" Debbie asked. Janet was pretty sure she was the only one who heard what Debbie was really asking.

"Yep," Ethan said. "It's another reason I don't want to miss celebrating his life next week. I wouldn't have missed it anyway, but to miss it after his gift has literally changed my life would be disrespectful to his memory."

"I should say so," Janet said.

"Well, anyway, we should let you get back to work. And Brendan, please tell your mother I said hello."

"Sure thing, Debbie."

As they walked away, Debbie asked Janet, "Do we believe him? An inheritance from his grandfather?"

"I don't know," Janet said. "He was excited to tell us about his grandfather giving it to him. It's kind of weird to be so open about money, isn't it?"

"Maybe it's a generational thing," Debbie said. "Like the engagement without the ring."

"Maybe." Janet hoped Tiffany didn't go around telling people how much money she had. Then again, she didn't have a lot, so there was that. The ring on Rachel's finger and the car Ethan drove said that he had money, even if he didn't say the words out loud.

"What do you think about the timing?" Debbie asked.

"If he'd said his grandfather had passed away more recently, it would be harder to believe, but I suppose the estate could have been settled by now."

"Is he really from Connecticut?" Debbie asked.

"I don't know, but it shouldn't be too hard to find out whether a relative of Ethan Meyers died in Westport, Connecticut. He would be listed as a surviving relative in the obituary, I would think."

"Probably," Debbie agreed. "It would be a good place to start anyway."

CHAPTER SIXTEEN

Not long after Janet got home, the thunderheads that had gathered along the horizon let loose, and heavy raindrops splattered against the pavement. Janet went out and stood on the porch, watching the rain fall in sheets. She loved a good summer thunderstorm, and she took a deep breath of the sweet air and enjoyed the feel of the cooling breeze on her skin. When the rain started to lessen, she reluctantly went back inside and decided it was time to figure out dinner.

Ian and Tiffany had both texted to say they expected to be home in time for the meal, so Janet decided to make kabobs. They could be grilled outside, so she wouldn't have to use the oven. She whipped up a marinade and then chopped chicken into small pieces, which she threaded onto skewers along with chunks of peppers, new potatoes, red onion, tomato, and Halloumi cheese. She set them in the marinade and made a green salad. Then she poured herself a glass of lemonade.

She sat on the cooled porch and read her book. But the question about Ethan's inheritance nagged at her. If it was true, it could explain how he had come into such a seemingly large amount of money. She decided to do a quick bit of research to see if she could verify his story. She sat down at the table with her laptop. Ranger jumped into her lap, and she stroked his furry head.

She started by searching *Westport, Connecticut,* to see if they had a local paper. She quickly discovered that Westport was a wealthy town on the Long Island Sound, filled with large homes and a quaint downtown. It had a nice yacht club, several golf courses, and scenic, leafy streets. She clicked on a real estate ad and got distracted for a while admiring the sights. A lovely colonial sat on half an acre, with a gracious dining room, a sleek kitchen with marble counters, a pool, and a—

Was that the right price? Surely there was an extra zero in there.

Apparently, that was the right price. Janet quickly closed the real estate site. She wouldn't be buying a home in Westport anytime soon, that was for sure. For now, she needed to focus on the search for Ethan's grandfather.

It wasn't hard to find the website of the *Westport Journal.* She clicked on the Obituaries button at the top of the page and scanned the recent entries.

Frances Hyman had been ninety, and there was a lovely photo of her with bobbed hair from a few decades before. She had been very involved in raising money for various children's causes in the area. Below her was an obituary for Robert Gill, who'd been seventy-six and had worked on Wall Street.

As much as she enjoyed reading the details of the lives of people she'd never known, Janet realized it would take her hours if she went through them one at a time. She did a search for *Ethan Meyers* and quickly uncovered the obituary for a Milton Glaser, who had passed away in March. That checked out with what Ethan had said.

She scanned the article. He'd apparently been an investment specialist and a bird-watching enthusiast, and he'd been very involved with charitable efforts in Westport and the surrounding area. His sole surviving relatives appeared to be his grandsons. He had been predeceased by his wife and daughter, Rosemary. Rosemary's husband and Ethan's father, Cooper, was mentioned, and Ethan Meyers was listed as one of the three surviving grandchildren.

She hadn't known Ethan's mother was gone. She felt for him, to have lost a parent already. And though his father was still alive, he hadn't gotten any of the inheritance. It had all passed to the grandchildren.

It made sense. Given what she'd learned, it did seem likely that if Milton had divided his money between his three grandsons, Ethan had likely inherited a sizable amount of money.

That didn't prove that he'd had nothing to do with the fire at the warehouse. But it did give a plausible explanation for how he'd recently come into money. It wasn't impossible that he had been paid to pass along the key to the warehouse, but it now seemed far less likely that he'd needed the money badly enough to be tempted.

Janet leaned back in her chair. She didn't know whether to be disappointed or relieved about the inheritance. The last thing she wanted was for a member of Ian's squad to have been involved in the crime. Based on what she saw here and the explanation he'd given her, she could cross Ethan off her list.

But if Ethan hadn't taken or given the key to someone to get into the cage, how had the arsonist gotten in? Ian hadn't done it, which meant that one of the other officers must have taken the key and either broken in or passed the key to whoever had. But who? Brendan? Captain Hernandez? She couldn't imagine it, and she knew Ian couldn't either.

She thought about the suspects still on her list. Jennie Ward, Todd Mills, and Austin and Tyler Wilson. She'd already pretty much decided that Jedidiah Merrick wouldn't have set fire to his own gun. As far as she knew, none of the others had a clear connection to anyone on the police force. There were so many question marks around the Wilsons—the baseball bat, the gum wrapper, the fact that at least one of them had most likely lied about his whereabouts on Tuesday night. And Austin had known about the fire starting in the cage, even though that wasn't public knowledge.

Then there was Todd Mills. Ian hadn't thought that the contractor was a likely suspect. And, really, he paled in comparison to the others. Charges of driving under the influence or arson struck Janet as stronger motives than Todd had.

She'd already researched him online and doubted she would find anything more there. Still, she had some time, and she really wanted answers, so she tried again.

She started with a more general web search, but she found the same results she'd gotten last time. She'd already found the information about Todd on the county clerk's site, so this time she decided to check the archives of the *Gazette* for any mention of Todd in the newspaper. That search returned nothing.

She clicked to the website for the New Philadelphia *Times Reporter*, and this time she found a marriage announcement dated nearly twenty years before.

Todd Travis Mills married Dana Elizabeth Whittaker Saturday at 1 pm at Sacred Heart Catholic Church in New Philadelphia. The bride, daughter of Matthew and Diane

Whittaker, is from New Philadelphia, where her father is a doctor. The groom is the son of Jerry and Elaine Mills, who own a contracting company, and hails from Columbus. The couple will reside in Dennison.

There was also a photo of a much younger Todd beside a brown-haired woman with a broad smile.

Todd had said his wife was from the area and that was why they lived there. Janet decided to see if she could learn anything more about his wife. She ran a search for *Dana Mills* and quickly found a social media site that showcased plenty of photos of a Victorian house in the rural countryside. It was the same house she'd seen featured on Todd's website. This was the right Dana. Janet scrolled through the photos. In addition to the house, a brood of chickens and some baby goats were featured on the site, along with pictures of a lush garden and a boy who was probably in middle school, if she had to guess.

Janet clicked on one of the photos of the boy. He had brown hair and freckles and appeared to be in a soccer uniform. *Shane living his best life*, read the caption. Several comments talked about how big Shane was getting and how handsome he was.

Janet scrolled, clicking on more photos of Shane. There was a picture of him graduating from his local elementary school, several of him playing various sports, one with some friends at a lake, and one of him in a soccer uniform standing in what Janet recognized as the foyer of their home. On Todd's site, the foyer had been perfectly clean, with the frame focused on the herringbone flooring. In this photo, the entryway was crowded with the detritus of family life—coats and sweaters and cleats and athletic bags. Janet scrolled for a while, and though she was glad to learn more about Todd's life and family, she knew she wouldn't find anything about the case here.

The other suspect still on her list was Jennie Ward. Janet still thought Jennie was a very likely suspect. Even ignoring the fact that she'd threatened Janet and Debbie, she had an arson charge, and she had every reason to want the evidence of her past crime to disappear. There had to be more Janet could find out about Jennie.

Her fingers hovered over the keyboard as she considered where to search. She decided to read the transcription of Jennie's arraignment again to refresh her memory. She went back to the court clerk's website and found the document she'd read before, the court stenographer's record.

Jennie had taken out a large insurance policy on the house mere weeks before it burned down. This time, Janet noticed a detail she'd missed the first time through—Jennie had bought the insurance from Barry Smith, Kim Smith's husband. That made sense, as he was one of the few insurance brokers in town. Janet couldn't see how that was relevant, so she kept reading.

When she got to the end of the transcription, Janet realized something. She'd noticed the first time through that the transcription ended abruptly, but she hadn't thought much of it. But now she saw that it didn't simply end. There were numbers at the bottom of the pages, and the last page in the document was page eight of thirteen. This wasn't the entire transcript. Where was the rest of it?

She went back to the clerk's website and reran her search, but all she got was the same partial document. Why weren't the rest of the pages included? Was it an oversight—or was there a reason the public was being shielded from whatever was in the rest of the transcript?

Janet didn't know. But she had an idea how she could find out.

When Ian came home, Janet had already checked the hours for the New Philadelphia courthouse and made a plan to head there the next day after work. Then she'd gotten the grill going and greeted Ian when he stepped inside.

He kissed her cheek, but it was clear to her that he was wound up, and he couldn't seem to relax as she grilled the kabobs. Tiffany wasn't home yet and hadn't called to say when she would be back. She could reheat dinner if she wanted when she arrived.

"Can you tell me about it?" Janet asked after the kabobs were plated and they'd said grace.

Ian took a bite, and as he chewed, he sat back in his chair. "I can tell you this," he finally said. "You were right."

"Of course I was." She used her fork to scoot the grilled veggies, meat, and cheese off the skewer. "About what?"

"About Jennie Ward hiding something on her property. We got a search warrant to go on it—"

"I thought that wasn't easy to do." And on a Sunday no less. That did explain what had kept Ian so busy though.

"It's not, but we found our angle. We had her on our radar anyway, because her boyfriend has a couple of arrests for theft."

"What did he steal?"

"Cars. We had evidence he was running a chop shop, but we didn't know where. We'd flown drones over the property, but nothing was out in the open. There's an old building on the property, way out in the woods. It was probably used for hunting at some point. We'd seen it in aerial shots of the area, so we knew it was there, but without access to it, we couldn't see if it was what we thought it might be. With your tip about the camera, though, we got a judge to give us permission to search Jennie's property. And we found it. They had hundreds of thousands of dollars' worth of car parts."

"So what you're saying is that it's a good thing Debbie and I went out there." Janet gave him her brightest smile.

"I wouldn't say that, exactly," Ian said. "Being threatened by someone with a cache of guns isn't exactly the kind of situation I'd want my wife in."

"I'll take that as a thank-you and say you're welcome."

"Unfortunately, it still doesn't tell us whether she was behind the warehouse fire," he said.

"It doesn't," Janet agreed. "But listen to this. I chatted with Austin at the festival, and he mentioned the fact that the fire had started in the cage inside the warehouse, and I wasn't sure how he knew that. You told me it wasn't public knowledge and that almost no one knew, so I wasn't sure how he did."

Ian set his fork down. "He knew about the cage?"

"He mentioned it. I didn't ask how he knew."

"I'm glad you didn't," he said. "We'll check that out."

"And for what it's worth, Carrie told me Austin was working at the hospital Tuesday night, but today at church Tyler said Austin had taken the whole week off. I'm sure you verified his alibi—"

"Carrie told you Austin was working Tuesday night?" Ian cocked his head. "She told us he was at home, and Austin told us he was home too."

"They're giving us different stories?" Janet asked. Was her friend confused—or had she intentionally lied to Janet?

She couldn't imagine Carrie lying. But then, she had the strongest motivation of all, to protect someone she loved. If she lied about where Austin had been, it would have been to give him an alibi. Could she have simply been confused about his schedule? But how could that be, when he'd taken the whole week off?

Or was it Carrie who'd set the fire? She also had access to the bat and the gum, and she had the motivation. But Janet couldn't see it. She knew Carrie pretty well, and she couldn't imagine that.

Which brought her back to her main question. "Why would Carrie tell me that if it wasn't true?"

"People lie for all kinds of reasons," Ian said. "If she thought you suspected her husband, she could have invented an alibi for him. But lying to the police is a much bigger deal, so maybe she decided to be straight with us. Or maybe she was confused when she spoke with you. It's hard to say."

Though she was glad to hear Carrie had told the police the truth, it still stung to find out that her friend had likely lied to her. Thinking back on the conversation, Janet didn't think Carrie had been confused.

"In any case, Austin's alibi is that he was home with his wife, and we have no way to prove or disprove it. Honestly, it would have been better for him if he had been at work, where more people who were less likely to be biased in his favor would be able to confirm it.

But with his wife to vouch for him—and with the question mark about whether she was telling the truth, since we know she told you something different—there's still no way to know if that's really where he was or not. Carrie's alibi also rests on Austin, so we'd have to prove one of them lied to make any progress there."

"What about Tyler?"

"Tyler's alibi checks out," Ian said. "The manager at the theater says he saw him there when the movie was over. He went to the 3D showing, which was at seven thirty, like Carrie said. The worker you talked to only looked at the 2D showings from Tuesday." So that was another name crossed off the list.

Slowly, the list was getting smaller. They would figure out who did it soon. Janet could sense it.

CHAPTER SEVENTEEN

Cincinnati, Ohio
1970

Mama,

I've arrived in Cincinnati, safe and sound, and rented a nice apartment over a family with a couple of small kids. They remind me of Dino and Delilah, though their mother is younger than Seelie. I've gotten a job working for a big household goods company and am using my money from the army to take classes at night. I should have my business degree in a couple of years.

Nicky wrote to me that the old train station in Dennison doesn't take passenger trains anymore. They finally gave up trying to get people to go to that little town, I guess. I am sorry to hear it though.

Enclosed is $10 for you from my first paycheck.
Don't worry about me. I'm on my way, and I'm not
looking back.
    John

Janet hoped Monday would start slowly after the busy weekend, but they had a steady stream of customers from the time the doors opened. Janet did her best to make every one of them feel welcome. She chatted with the regulars and was particularly glad to see Harry and Crosby.

"Did your friend find you?" Janet asked as he finished his breakfast.

Harry took a sip of coffee. "I wouldn't say John Milken is my friend, and no, I haven't come across his path yet."

"He's not?" *Why would he be trying to find Harry then?*

"I wouldn't say he was. Truth be told, he was pretty awful to me. I'm not too bothered if he doesn't find me. I don't have much to say to him."

Janet waited for him to explain, but Harry merely thanked her for breakfast then left with Crosby.

"John Milken isn't his friend?" Debbie was frothing milk and had heard the whole exchange.

"I guess not." Janet wasn't sure what to make of it. "I can't believe it. I've never heard of Harry not being friends with someone."

"I was concerned that they hadn't found each other yet, but maybe it's for the best," Debbie murmured.

Janet looked out at the train platform, where Harry slowly lowered himself down onto the bench, Crosby at his feet. What had happened between Harry and John Milken?

When Patricia came in, Janet asked her about it.

"I don't know who John Milken is," Patricia said. "But Pop Pop has been upset ever since he heard this guy was in town."

"Oh dear. I'm so sorry I tried to connect them."

"It's not your fault," Patricia said, accepting her peppermint mocha to go. "He'll tell us what's going on when he's ready."

Janet waved as Patricia walked out the door, but as soon as she was gone, Janet realized something. Patricia was representing the museum in the case against Todd Mills. She wondered if Patricia would be able to tell her anything about the contractor that would shed light on whether he might have had something to do with the fire at the warehouse. For a brief moment, she considered running after her but quickly decided against it. She had a business to run, after all. But maybe she would find another time to talk to Patricia about Todd.

The workday passed quickly. As they finished the process of closing for the day, Janet asked Debbie if she wanted to come with her.

Debbie wrinkled her nose. "To the courthouse? To dig around in boring old paperwork?"

"The paperwork is not especially old."

"My objection was to it being boring, not its age. At least old documents can be rather interesting. You never know what you might find. But modern paperwork is so sterile."

"I'll take that as a no."

"Are you nuts? Of course I'm in. It might not be my idea of a good time, but I'm not leaving you to solve this case alone now."

Feeling a bit of whiplash, Janet said, "I don't know that it's going to help me solve the case."

"You wouldn't be doing it if you didn't think there was a chance. Your car or mine?"

They hopped in Janet's car and drove to New Philadelphia, the county seat. The courthouse was a grand limestone building with a Classical Revival facade and a huge copper dome. They parked along the side of the building and followed signs to a side entrance that directed them to the office of the clerk of courts. Inside, they followed signs down a hallway and to an office with a glass door. A young woman sat behind the counter and smiled at them as they walked inside.

"Here about jury duty?" She had shoulder-length brown hair and big brown eyes, and she seemed eager to help.

Janet shook her head. "Not today."

"Is that why most people come here?" Debbie asked.

She laughed. "Ninety percent are here trying to get *out* of jury duty. What can I help you with?"

"We're hoping to see the files for an upcoming court case," Janet said. "I read the arraignment online, but it seemed to have pages missing."

"That's not supposed to happen. I'll pull the physical file. I'll just need you to fill out this form." She slid a clipboard of forms across the desk and gestured toward a cup of pens.

"Sure thing." Janet grabbed a pen and filled in her name and address, the name of at least one person involved, and her reason for requesting the file. *Curiosity,* she wrote. She held the clipboard out, and the woman took it.

She nodded. "Yep. I know this case. I'll be right back. If you want to have a seat at one of the desks there, I'll bring it out to you." She indicated a cluster of tables in the open area in front of the counter.

"Thank you."

Janet and Debbie took a seat in the plastic chairs. Once the woman had disappeared, Debbie whispered, "Do you think it's a bad thing that she knows exactly which case Jennie is involved in?"

"I'm not sure," Janet said. "It could mean any number of things, I guess."

"But how many of those things could be good?"

Janet shrugged. "It could be good for us."

Then Janet had another idea. She went back to the woman's desk and retrieved the clipboard. She filled out another form to request the records for the depot's lawsuit filed against Todd Mills. It couldn't hurt to see those either, in case anything had been missing online.

The woman returned a few minutes later with a manila folder. "You're free to review the file here, but it can't leave this room."

"We understand," Debbie said.

"Can we actually see one more file as well?" Janet asked as she took the folder.

"Sure thing." The woman took the request form. "I'll be just a minute."

Janet opened the Jennie Ward file. Inside were several pieces of paper that seemed to be procedural instructions, and then she found the arraignment transcription—with the pages that had been omitted from the online version. "Jackpot."

She thumbed to page nine and read the pages that were new to her. The first page continued the judge's remarks about the fire, making sure Jennie was certain about her not-guilty plea. Jennie confirmed through her lawyer that she was. But then the judge had moved on to more charges. In addition to the arson, Jennie had been accused of trespassing and petty larceny.

"What did she steal?" Debbie asked, reading over her shoulder.

The legal mumbo jumbo made it hard to follow, but Janet understood the gist. "She's accused of sneaking onto a neighbor's farm and stealing gas from a storage tank. That's what she used to start the fire at her mom's place. Allegedly."

Many of the farmers in the area had fuel storage tanks on their property. They used the gasoline for tractors and other equipment. The gasoline delivery trucks came through every so often to refill the tanks.

"She didn't even buy her own gas before she used it to burn the place down?"

"Apparently not."

"Interesting." Debbie sat back. "Did the farmer report any gas being stolen recently?"

Janet saw what Debbie was getting at. "I don't know. But it does list the address of the property she's accused of stealing the gas from."

"Write it down. We can figure out who lives there and ask if them about it."

Janet recorded the address of the property as Debbie researched it on her phone.

The receptionist came back with the file she'd requested about the Todd Mills lawsuit. Janet skimmed it and saw that it was the same material she'd already read online. She set the file aside.

"Any luck on the homeowner of the address?" Janet asked.

"Nothing yet." Debbie kept scrolling. "Okay, how else can we figure out who lives there? Can we search the court files?"

"The county clerk's office would have property records," Janet said.

"Or there's an easier way to figure it out." Debbie had a familiar gleam in her eye.

"You want to go there, don't you?"

"Do you have anything else planned right now?"

"I can't say that I do," Janet admitted.

"Then let's go."

CHAPTER EIGHTEEN

Janet typed the address into her GPS, and twenty minutes later they bumped up the rutted dirt driveway of a farm about half a mile from the burned-out house that had belonged to Jennie's mom. STEVENS was painted neatly on the mailbox. A white farmhouse with a wraparound porch stood to the left of the driveway, shaded by oak trees and red maples. To the right of the driveway was a red barn with an American flag painted on the side, and a garden and chicken coop sat in front of it. The distant hum of a tractor rumbled in the still air.

Janet parked, and they walked up the steps to the porch and rang the doorbell. She heard movement inside, and then a young woman in cutoff shorts and a baggy blue T-shirt that read FIRECRACKER 5K 2018 answered the door.

"Hello," she said with a wary smile. "Can I help you?"

"I'm Janet Shaw," Janet said, "and this is Debbie Albright. Do you live here?"

"Yes," she said. Behind her, Janet could see a toddler using fingerpaints at a kitchen table.

"We heard about the gasoline that was stolen from your tank last year, and we were wondering if any more had been taken recently," Janet said.

"Are you with the police?" the young woman asked.

"We're not," Debbie said. "But we read that the gas that was stolen from your tank may have been used to start a fire. We're trying to figure out if it might have happened again."

"I see." She still eyed them warily. "Jared already spoke to the police. Anyway, the answer is no. When we reported the theft earlier—it wasn't the first time it had happened. We didn't want to call the cops on a neighbor if she was desperate, but it got to be where we couldn't afford the loss. Fuel is expensive, and farmers don't make much money to begin with, as I'm sure you know."

"Did you know who it was stealing the gas?" Janet asked.

"We have a camera out there," the woman said. "We installed it after the first time, and every time the gas was taken after that, it was the same person."

"That was Jennie Ward?"

"Yes." She nodded. "She lives up the road. She's always been funny. Not too friendly, keeps to herself. With everything going on with her mom, we thought she had hit some hard times and looked the other way as long as we could. But like I said, after a while it got too expensive for us to ignore. Jared went over and told her we'd seen her on camera. He tried to reason with her, but she denied it and screamed in his face to get off her property. That's when we reported the theft."

"And no gas has been taken since?"

"No."

Janet tried to think of what else to ask her, but all her questions had been answered. "Thanks so much for your time." She fought the urge to tell the woman to enjoy this precious time with her toddler, because it would go by too quickly. She'd hated it when people said things like that to her when Tiffany was little. But it was true.

Back in the car, Janet asked, "So what do you think?"

"It would have been nice if they'd had gas taken recently," Debbie said.

"I don't know that I would say it would be nice. Convenient for us, maybe. But definitely not for them."

"You know what I mean. It would be nice if we could make a clear connection to Jennie. But even if she didn't steal gas from them for the warehouse fire, she could still have been involved."

"I agree." Janet pulled out of the bumpy driveway and steered onto the road. "This didn't implicate her, but it didn't eliminate her either."

"Which is not really helpful." Debbie folded her arms over her chest. "So what now? Do you have any other thoughts about how we could prove it was Jennie—or anyone else, for that matter?"

Janet shook her head. "No. I wish I did. But I do want to learn more about the Todd Mills lawsuit."

The next intersection was for State Route 36. After stopping for a pickup loaded with outdoor furniture, they continued toward town.

"You didn't learn anything new when you looked in the file?"

"No. It had all the same stuff that was online."

"Do you have any ideas on how we could find out more about him?"

"Yes, actually, I do." She turned onto the main road. "Patricia is representing the museum in the suit against Todd Mills. I'm wondering if she could tell us more about exactly what evidence was stored in the warehouse and whether its absence might make it more difficult to win the case against him. Are you okay with making another stop before we head back?"

"I wouldn't miss it."

Patricia's office was in a storefront of one of the historic brick buildings along North 2nd Street. Her door was labeled Patricia Franklin, Attorney-at-Law.

Janet pushed the door open and stepped into the lobby area, which held leather club chairs and an Oriental rug over hardwood floors. Big windows let in plenty of sunlight. A dark wooden antique desk stood at the back wall, and Janet smiled when she saw Patricia's mother, Ruth, sitting behind the desk.

"Hello, Ruth."

"Hello, Janet. Debbie." Patricia's mom had retired from her job as a dietician and now worked part-time for Patricia. She was a slender woman with big glasses and an easy smile. "It's nice to see you both."

"It's good to see you too," Janet said. "How's Vernon?"

"My husband is as fine as can be. Enjoying that pool we put in this summer, I can tell you that. He's been out there every day in this heat. I think he's part fish at this point."

"I can imagine," Debbie said. "It sounds heavenly."

"It does feel wonderful," Ruth said. "Now, what can I help you two with?"

"We were hoping Patricia might have a moment to answer a question for us," Janet said.

"Let me check with the boss," Ruth said with a grin. She walked down the hallway and opened Patricia's office door. After a few moments of quiet conversation, Ruth returned. "She's free. Come on back."

She ushered them into Patricia's office.

"Hello, you two." Patricia typed something into her computer then smiled up at them. "What's going on?" She gestured for them to sit in the stylish leather chairs across from her desk.

"Hi, Patricia," Janet said, taking a seat. "Thanks so much for seeing us. We have a few questions we're hoping you might be able to help with."

"I'll do my best. Is it something to do with the café?"

"No," Debbie said. "Not exactly."

"It's about the lawsuit between the depot museum and Todd Mills," Janet explained.

"There's not much I can share about that," Patricia said. "It's an active case, and I prioritize my clients' confidentiality."

"We know you can't tell us anything specific," Janet said. "I've read the lawsuit you filed on the clerk of courts website, so I have a general idea of what the charges are and why the suit is being brought."

"You read that?" Patricia looked impressed.

"I did my best. Legalese is not my specialty."

"It's almost as if they want to make it impossible for anybody who isn't a lawyer to understand." Patricia chuckled.

Janet laughed. "That's true. But I did make out that he's been accused of fraud, gross negligence, and breach of contract."

"That's right."

"Can you tell us what he did exactly that led to each of the charges?"

"I'm afraid I can't." Patricia cocked her head. "Why do you want to know?"

Janet hesitated. She wasn't sure how much to say. "I discovered he's been accused of pretty much the same charges for other projects he's worked on."

"I can't comment on other cases either," Patricia said. "Not so much for the confidentiality reason as that my comments could be taken as legal advice, and I'm careful not to do that for cases I'm not involved in."

"There sure seems to be a pattern emerging of shoddy work and pocketing the customers' money for himself," Debbie said.

"I'm not arguing with you, but I also can't officially confirm or deny your conclusion," Patricia said.

Janet knew Patricia was doing her job, and she respected her for it, as frustrating as it was. No one wanted a lawyer who went around gossiping—whether about their own cases or someone else's.

Janet decided to cut to the chase. "We were really hoping to find out more about the evidence against Todd stored in the warehouse that burned down Tuesday night. There was evidence for the case in the warehouse, right?"

"That is where evidence for upcoming trials is stored," Patricia said carefully.

"I see," Janet said. "If that evidence was gone, would there still be a case against Todd?"

Patricia leaned back in her leather desk chair. She didn't answer for minute. Then, slowly, she said, "As I said, I can't speak about the details of a case."

"Obviously, if the evidence was destroyed in the fire, that would make it more challenging to win any case." Janet didn't want to come out and say Todd was a suspect in the warehouse fire, but she assumed Patricia understood.

"Do you have reason to assume he might have been involved with the fire at the warehouse?" Patricia asked.

"It's been suggested that he might have been," Janet said, choosing her words carefully.

"I see." Patricia examined her cuff. "I was informed by the Dennison Police Department that the evidence we submitted for our case is no longer available, so it cannot be used in court." She hadn't said it had been burned in the fire, but that was what she'd meant. "Which is a setback for us. If there wasn't more evidence available that would prove our case, I might be more concerned than I am. As it is, my stress level is very manageable right now."

"So more evidence against Todd does exist?"

"I couldn't discuss something like that with someone who isn't my client," Patricia said. "But I can tell you I'm confident that we'll still win."

So there *was* more evidence against Todd somewhere. Did he know that? If so, it gave less credence to the idea that he might have set the fire. It was a lot of trouble and effort for him to have gone to if it would destroy only part of the evidence against him.

"Can you tell us where that evidence might be?" Janet asked.

"I cannot," Patricia said.

It seemed like Patricia couldn't tell them anything they wanted to know, but Janet had anticipated something like that. She couldn't ask her friend to compromise her professional integrity.

"Well, thank you for your time," Janet said. "We appreciate it." She stood, and Debbie followed suit beside her.

Patricia nodded but didn't move. Then, slowly, deliberately, she said, "I hope you're able to unlock the truth of this case."

"Thank you," Debbie said. "We hope so too."

Patricia walked them to the front of the office. They said goodbye to Ruth and then headed back outside.

"What was that about?" Janet said when they were standing on the sidewalk.

"I think she legitimately couldn't talk to us about the case," Debbie said.

"I got that," Janet said. "But what was the whole thing about unlocking the case? Was that significant somehow?"

Debbie shrugged. "I thought she was wishing us luck."

"Maybe. But it sounded to me like she was trying to say something without saying it."

"What do you think she could have meant?"

"I don't know."

Debbie laughed. "Well, let's ponder that, I guess. In the meantime, we should focus on the suspects still in the running."

"I guess so."

Janet went home and got to work on dinner—fried chicken and mashed potatoes—but something nagged at the back of her mind. It felt important, but she couldn't drag it to the surface. She tried to figure it out as she worked on dinner, but whatever it was stayed buried.

She raised her head as Tiffany walked in smelling like sunscreen and chlorine. "Hi. How was work?"

"Boring," Tiffany said. She kicked off her flip-flops and set her bag down. "But that's a good thing for a lifeguard. It means no one drowned."

"I'm glad to hear it." Something was off with Tiffany again. She wasn't her usual chipper self. "What are your plans for tonight?"

"Hanging around here," Tiffany said. "Maybe I'll watch some TV."

"That sounds nice." Janet was delighted at the prospect of more time with her daughter. But she also had to ask, "Is everything all right?" Tiffany had been going out with her friends most nights this summer, so this was a little odd.

"Yeah," Tiffany said. She pulled her water bottle from her bag and took a long drink then set the bottle on the counter. She blew out a breath. "Things have gotten weird with the whole lake situation, and I don't really want to deal with it tonight."

Janet had been chopping onions, but she put her knife down. "What do you mean, things have gotten weird?"

"That kid, Liam, who Hudson knows? He's trying to make it into a party weekend. He's planning to bring alcohol and invite a bunch of people we don't know. Layla and I don't want it to be like that. We want to hang out with our friends and talk and swim, you know? Not deal with underage strangers who'll be drinking and doing who knows what else. So I said I wasn't sure if I wanted to go. Layla said the same thing, so now Hudson is kind of freaking out. He wants us to come, but he already invited Liam and doesn't want to tell him he can't come or that he can't bring his friends. I don't want Hudson to be mad at me, but I also don't want to be a part of something that stupid."

"That sounds complicated." Janet tried to keep her emotions in check when all she wanted to do was tell Tiffany not to go and simultaneously pump her fist on hearing that Tiffany didn't want to be involved if there was alcohol. She was only nineteen, as were her friends. "Is there anything I can do to help?"

"I don't think so," Tiffany said. "I wish things could go back to the way they were when we first talked about this. When it was me and Layla and Hudson going to play games and swim. I don't see why it has to be this other thing."

"I'm sorry, honey." Janet wanted to give Tiffany a hug, but her daughter's posture said she wasn't open to that, so Janet stayed put. "It sounds like you've talked to Hudson and he's unwilling or unable to make it what you originally thought it would be."

"Exactly. He's nervous about standing up to Liam, which tells me Liam isn't the kind of friend Hudson needs to have around in the first place. But I don't get to decide that for him. I made the mistake of telling him what I thought, and now things are awkward between us. I just wish the whole thing had never happened And I don't know what to do now. I don't want to lose my friendship with Hudson over a stupid thing like this."

Janet fought the urge to tell Tiffany what she wanted her to do. Tiffany hadn't asked for her input, so Janet needed to give her the space to make the decision on her own. She had raised Tiffany to think for herself, so she would do no good by trying to take over now.

She chose her words carefully. "What would help you make your decision?"

Tiffany took a deep breath. "I think I need to not think about it for a while, then maybe come back to it when I feel fresher. I'm going to go take a shower."

"I think that's wise. And I'm here if you need me."

"I know." Tiffany gave her a small smile and headed out of the kitchen.

Janet watched her go. It was so hard to know how to help Tiffany through situations like this. Naturally, Janet didn't want her to go to a cabin where kids would be drinking. If this had happened two years before, Janet could have put her foot down. But things were different now, and she wasn't sure how she was supposed to act to best help her daughter. She would always be Tiffany's mom. She would always worry about her and want to guide her, and it was scary and exciting to watch her grow more independent all the time. She had to support Tiffany's autonomy, even when she wanted to fix everything for her. She'd seen far too many parents who'd tried to control their children's lives for too long. When their children moved out, they had no idea how to think for themselves and made bad choices.

So Janet prayed. She prayed that Tiffany would make good decisions and that she would seek to glorify the Lord in all she did. She also prayed that God would guide her own actions to best support her daughter.

Ian called to say he would be working late. When Tiffany came into the kitchen for dinner, Janet waited for her to bring up her dilemma again. She didn't, so Janet assumed Tiffany still needed the mental break from it. They chatted about something that had happened at the pool, and then they watched TV together. Then Janet went to bed, hoping a good night's sleep would help her make sense of everything that was tangled up in her head.

But she didn't get a good night's sleep. She sat straight up in bed around three in the morning as it finally came to her. She realized the thing that had been bothering her earlier.

The gas used to start the fire. She had a good idea where it had come from.

CHAPTER NINETEEN

*J*anet nudged her sleeping husband. "Ian."

Ian rolled over with a groan. "What?"

"The gas for the fire. Did you check if it came from the RV?"

"What RV?" His eyes blinked open. Light from the streetlamp outside filtered in through the narrow slits in the blinds, making him squint.

"Out on Route 36. When Debbie and I were in the station, someone called to report gas stolen from an RV. Do you think someone stole it to start the fire?"

Ian sat up on his elbows. "Why would someone do that?"

"Well, they needed to take gasoline to the warehouse to start the fire. And they knew that if they bought it at a gas station, someone might remember them doing that. So they siphoned it out of the RV to avoid being seen buying a container of gas."

Ian frowned. "But why wouldn't the arsonist just siphon it from their own car? Why take the chance they might get caught stealing gas?"

Janet's shoulders slumped. "Oh. That's a good point." She thought for a minute. "But maybe they didn't have very much gas left in their car and needed it to get to the warehouse. Or maybe they don't have a car because it was inside the warehouse when it burned."

"If they didn't have a car, how would they get to the scene of the fire?" Ian sounded exhausted. "It's not a bad theory, Janet, but it doesn't seem very likely to me."

Janet realized she had to be more direct. "What about Jennie Ward? Didn't she steal the gas she used to start the fire at her mom's place?"

"It hasn't been proven that's where the gas for that fire came from," Ian said. "But we already talked to the farmer whose gas she took, and he reported no gas had been taken from his tank recently."

"Right. Because she moved on to taking it from the RV instead," Janet said.

"I had an officer check out the RV call," Ian said. "The timing doesn't work, Janet. The gas wasn't siphoned off until Wednesday. That was the day after the fire. So, again, it's not a bad theory, but it doesn't seem likely in this case."

Ian kissed her cheek and then lay back and rolled over. Within moments, the even sound of his breathing told her he'd fallen asleep.

Janet lay awake for another hour, thinking through the conversation, turning it over in her mind, wondering about it.

Something didn't add up. She replayed what she'd overheard Veronica say at the police station. Was Ian was wrong about the timing? Should she wake him up and tell him? She was pretty sure he wouldn't appreciate that. Besides, she had to be at the café in just a few hours. She decided it could wait.

When Debbie came into the kitchen on Tuesday morning, Janet had blueberry and peach scones in the oven and was mixing the batter for the day's muffins. But as soon as she spotted her friend, Janet dropped her spoon and said, "I was thinking about the RV."

"Good morning to you too." Debbie smiled. "How was your night?"

"Fine and dandy," Janet said. "But listen. Remember when we were at the police station last week?"

"It was the highlight of my week." Debbie set her purse down and slipped an apron over her head. "It's not often I get to hear a drunk man threaten to sue the police. It ranks right up there with being threatened by a crazy lady, which, by the way, was a highlight of my weekend."

"Okay, so it's been an interesting week. But do you remember the phone call Veronica took while we waited for Ian?"

Debbie thought while she tied the apron strings behind her back. "She got one about a stolen bike, I think."

"Yes," Janet said. "But that's not the one I'm thinking of. There was a call about an RV."

Debbie pursed her lips then said, "Okay, yeah, I think I remember something about that."

"I didn't realize at first what it was about," Janet said. "But it kept nagging at me, and last night I finally figured it out. Someone called to report gas being stolen from their RV."

"You got that out of what you overheard at the police station?" Debbie shook her head. "I didn't get that."

"I did," Janet said. "I talked to Ian about it last night, but he said the timing didn't work out. He said the gas was siphoned out of the RV on Wednesday, which was the day after the fire. But I'm pretty sure what the caller actually said was that it could have been any time since the previous Sunday."

"You think the police got it wrong?"

"I don't know." Ian and his team rarely got things wrong. "Maybe they got more information?" But what she remembered hearing didn't match what Ian had said. "Something doesn't sit right with me. Something doesn't line up. Also, Veronica said it had happened on Route 36."

"You paid much closer attention than I did. I was clearly too focused on the drunk guy shouting."

"Route 36 is out by where Jennie Ward lives," Janet said.

"That road goes for miles. How do you know it happened near where Jennie lives?"

"Okay, I don't. But it probably is."

"How do you figure?"

"Jennie didn't steal gas from the farm tank this time," Janet said. "She knew they had a camera set up and she would be caught. So she found another place to steal it from."

"An RV parked in a yard," Debbie filled in for her. "It wouldn't be hard to siphon gas from that in the middle of the night."

"Not if you know what you're doing," Janet said.

"Which I do not, but Jennie might," Debbie said. "So what do we do now? Go out to her place and ask her?"

"I think the more reasonable thing to do would be to talk to the person who reported the gas stolen from the RV."

"Won't Ian be upset if we do that?" Debbie asked.

He probably wouldn't be thrilled, but technically they wouldn't be interfering in the case. "He's already investigated and dismissed the possible link," she said. "But what the investigating officer reported doesn't match what I remember. I think it would be okay to go and see if we can find out if I'm remembering right or not."

"Okay," Debbie said. "Do you know who it was or how to find the RV?"

"Veronica said it's on a corner by a creek," Janet said. "It has a big sycamore and a nice front porch."

"So we drive up and down Route 36 until we find a place matching that description?" Debbie asked.

"It would have an RV in the yard," Janet said. "How hard can it be to find?"

Debbie laughed. "Okay, I'm game. After work?"

"Sounds good to me."

Debbie chuckled. "To be clear, I didn't say it was a good plan. But it is a plan."

Tuesday was a bit slower than usual, and Janet was glad. Harry came in, Crosby walking alongside him. They chatted for a few minutes while Harry ate breakfast. Then he got a cup of coffee to go and sat on the bench on the platform.

John Milken came in a few minutes later.

"Back again?" Janet asked.

John smiled. "It's hard to stay away from coffee this good. And I'm going to miss those muffins when I go home."

"When are you heading home?" Janet asked, pouring some of the rich dark brew into a to-go cup.

"A few more days, probably. Depends on Mom. I run my own business, so I'm lucky to be able to work from wherever I want."

"That's really nice." She snapped the lid on the cup and held it out to him. "Is your mom doing better?"

"Getting there," he said. He took the cup from her. "Have you seen Harry Franklin this morning, by any chance?"

"He's out there." Janet pointed toward the platform before she could second-guess herself. Besides, she knew Harry wouldn't want her to lie for him.

"I was hoping I would catch him today. Thank you." John took his coffee and his bagged muffin and left the café.

Since no one was else in line, Janet walked around the counter and over to the window to watch John make his way slowly down the platform.

As he approached, Harry raised his head. Recognition flashed across his face, followed by something darker. Obviously sensing his owner's distress, Crosby stood and placed himself between Harry and this newcomer.

John stood awkwardly in front of Harry and spoke with an earnest expression.

"Are you spying?" Debbie asked from the doorway into the kitchen.

"I'm just monitoring the situation, making sure everything is all right," Janet said.

"Call it whatever you want. You should know better than to do it without me." Debbie crossed the café to stand beside Janet. They watched as John wiped his hand under his eye then ducked his head.

Harry sat silently, staring at the other man, with a look of disbelief on his face.

When he finished talking, John bobbed his head and turned to go, but Harry said something, slowly pushed himself to his feet, and held out his hand. John smiled and shook it, and then Harry pulled him in for a hug. When the hug ended, John wiped his eyes again, said something more to Harry, and then walked away.

Harry sat back down, shaking his head.

"What was that about?" Debbie asked.

Janet shrugged. "Whatever it was, Harry seemed okay with it at the end, so I guess that's a good thing."

"Then I'm glad they finally found each other, as much as Harry didn't want that."

"Me too," Janet agreed.

Customers began to trickle in again. Janet was too busy frying hamburgers and assembling sandwiches to know that Harry and Crosby had come back into the café again—until she went out to the dining area to check on things.

"Hello again, Harry. Need more coffee?"

"No thank you," he said. "I wanted to let you all know what was going on out there, since I know you were curious." He raised an eyebrow at her, his ghost of a smile letting her know that he'd spotted her "monitoring."

"Oh. Well…" She couldn't deny it, especially since he'd seen her. "Yes."

"But since I doubt you could hear us—not for lack of trying—I figured I'd come fill you in."

"You saw us?" Debbie asked. "And here we thought we were being so discreet."

"You two are anything but subtle." Harry laughed. "But that's okay. You've been trying to connect us this whole time, so you deserve to hear the truth."

"It sure didn't seem like you were very happy about the prospect before, so I wasn't sure we should keep trying," Janet said.

"He came to apologize." Harry beamed, and Janet could practically see the weight fall off his shoulders. "Can you believe that? After all these years."

"That's wonderful," Janet said. "Don't feel like you have to talk about it if you don't want to, but you know we're dying to know."

Harry grinned at her. "John and I are from the same part of town. I'm older than he is, obviously. He's close to Vernon's age, but we knew each other because we went to the same church. I've known him since he was a boy," Harry explained. "He never really seemed content in Dennison. Got out of here as quick as he could. Joined up when he turned eighteen, even though the war was on. Nearly broke his mom's heart when he chose the jungles of Vietnam over staying here with her."

"She must have been so worried." Janet was concerned about Tiffany going away with friends for the weekend. She couldn't imagine how it would feel to have a child go off to war.

"I know she was. She showed up at every prayer meeting in the weeks leading up to his departure, asking the Lord to change his mind, terrified that she was going to lose her son. Naturally she worried, though it was a noble thing he did, stepping up to fight when few were willing. But at the same time, he always had the attitude that he couldn't wait to get out of this town, no matter where he ended up."

"That must have been hard for his mom," Janet said.

"It was. And maybe I overstepped, but when he showed up to board the train to ship out, I told him that we'd all be praying for him and waiting for his safe return."

Janet knew that the last passenger train to stop in Dennison had been in 1968, so this must have happened in the early days of America's involvement in the war.

"He told me he was never coming back to this town and that the last thing he'd ever want was to end up like me, hoisting bags for people who didn't even know I existed."

Janet gasped. "He said that?"

"He did. I was a conductor by that point, but one of the porters had called in sick on my day off, so I'd volunteered to fill in for him. It was fun and nostalgic until my conversation with John. I didn't correct him about my job title, because it didn't matter. There's no shame in an honest job, no matter what it is."

"Oh my." Debbie looked as shocked as Janet felt. "How awful."

"I was pretty offended by his condescending words, I have to admit. I'd already put decades into my career, and I was proud of it, so it stung to have someone sneer at any part of it." Harry took a deep breath. "But he wasn't wrong, in some ways. The world was beginning to change for us. He really did have more opportunities than my generation had. He wasn't wrong to want to go after them."

"But he was wrong in how he expressed it," Janet replied.

"Indisputably. And sadly, he didn't change his tune over the years. He made it back from Vietnam and immediately went off to Cincinnati. After that, he rarely came home. When he did, he always had something to say to me about how I hadn't made anything of myself and how he was going to do better—and then how he was doing better. I never really understood why he chose to take it out on me. It was almost as if I represented all the forces that had tried to hold him back. Or maybe he was like that with everyone. I don't know. But he did go on to be quite a successful businessman in the end."

"That doesn't make up for belittling you," Debbie said, and Janet saw the same anger on her friend's face that she felt.

"No, it doesn't. Like I said, he rarely came into town, but when he did, I tried to avoid him as much as I could."

"I'm so sorry, Harry," Janet said.

"Though that explains why you didn't seem excited to see him," Debbie added.

"I wasn't going out of my way to miss him," Harry said. "But yeah, maybe I subconsciously tried to stay away from him, if I'm honest."

"So what happened?" Janet asked. "What changed that he apologized this morning?"

"From what he told me, it sounds like he found the Lord and has been in the process of apologizing to people he knows he's wronged," Harry said. "He listed off some of the hurtful things he'd said to me and then admitted there was probably more that he'd forgotten, even though he remembered more than I did. It would have been easy for him to let it go after all this time. He didn't have to come here to apologize, but the fact that he sought me out to do so—well, that takes courage."

"It does take courage to admit when we're wrong," Debbie agreed.

Harry didn't argue with that. "At first, when he started telling me how badly he'd wronged me, I wanted to say how right he was and how he should have known better. And that's when I realized I held bitterness in my heart."

"Of course you did," Janet said indignantly. "Who wouldn't, after all that?"

"But when he apologized, I realized I needed to let go of the bitterness I'd been holding on to," Harry said. "I was clinging to it like a security blanket, as if what he'd done let me believe he was somehow beyond redemption rather than a child of God. It did nothing but make my own hurt worse. I had to let that go, same as he had to admit what he'd done wrong."

"And just like that, your hurt is gone?" Debbie asked.

"No," Harry said. "I suspect it will take some time and a lot of prayer before I'm able to say I don't feel that anymore. Wounds leave scars after all. But the bitterness that's been festering in there for so long? I was able to let that go today. John Milken freed both of us in one conversation."

"I'm so glad," Janet told him.

"He also asked if there was anything he could do to help make it up to me."

"What did you say?" Debbie asked.

"I told him that his sins are forgiven, same as mine. That we all do hurtful things, and it's the blood of Jesus that washes us clean. I told him I forgave him and that I hoped he would know that he was a beloved child of God."

"Oh, Harry." Janet didn't know that she would have been able to be as gracious to someone who had treated her that way. "You're a better person than I am."

"No, I've simply lived longer," Harry said. "And I've seen enough to know that we all need grace."

Janet knew there was plenty of truth in what he said. She had seen, again and again, how the older people in her life demonstrated wisdom and modeled grace in ways she wished she could. She didn't know if it was because they had lived longer and survived more or whether they had acquired a special kind of insight over the years, but she hoped she would be able to live that kind of maturity someday. She also appreciated the reminder that though God was always the same, sometimes it was a good thing that people changed.

"That's very admirable," Debbie said, echoing Janet's thoughts.

"It was admirable of him to apologize." Harry finished his coffee and set his cup on the counter. "Thank you for telling him where to find me."

"Refill?" Janet asked.

"You know what?" Harry chuckled. "Why not? It's a special day."

"Go wild." As Janet poured him a second cup, she thought that it was a special day indeed.

CHAPTER TWENTY

After they'd closed and cleaned the café, Janet and Debbie headed out to the parking lot and climbed into Debbie's car. They hadn't even gotten to the outskirts of town when Debbie asked, "What's bothering you?"

"What do you mean?"

"Janet, we've been best friends for decades. I know when you're far away."

Janet sighed. "I suppose I am. I'm worried about Tiffany, honestly. Well, not exactly worried. I'm struggling to understand how best to interact with her right now. I know she's a grown adult, in college, and I've got to trust her to make good decisions. But I'm also worried about her, and I find myself wanting to swoop in and make decisions for her."

"I see," Debbie said. "You're trying to understand how to navigate the relationship now that she's not a kid anymore."

"I guess so. She's definitely no longer a child. And I'm trying to figure out what my role is in this phase of her life."

"She's in an interesting place," Debbie said. "Old enough to have lived on her own—"

"Not really on her own," Janet said. "In a dorm, with a room-mate and an RA on the floor, plus the whole infrastructure of the college making sure she's okay."

"Fine. Old enough to have lived away from her parents but not old enough to have made the leap to full independence. Though other people her age have done that if they don't go to college right after high school."

"That's true," Janet said. "I want her to have the freedom to make decisions about her own life, but at the same time, that's scary."

Debbie was quiet for a moment. "Listen," she said finally, "I don't have kids, so obviously I'm not an expert here. I know this is tough. But is it possible that you're not ready for her to be independent and you're having a hard time with how much she's grown up in the past year? And maybe, just maybe, you're scared she won't need you anymore?"

Janet was surprised when tears stung her eyes. She hadn't wanted to admit it to herself until Debbie said it out loud.

"Things are different from how they used to be," Debbie went on gently. "You and Ian had a lot more control over her life, and it's scary for anyone to let their kids go and allow them to make more of their own decisions."

Janet nodded as the tears spilled over.

"She's your little girl, Janet. She always will be. She'll always need you. But she's also not a little girl anymore. It's okay to be sad about that. But I guess I'd counsel you to enjoy the woman she's become, rather than miss it entirely because you're so caught up in how she's no longer a child. And that was the whole goal, remember? She was always going to grow up. She's pretty great—you know that, right?"

"She is." Janet couldn't argue with that.

"And she's got a good head on her shoulders. You and Ian have done a great job and still are. You'll figure this out together. And again, it's okay to be sad about how things have changed, as long as you make sure to enjoy where she is now too."

"Thanks," Janet said.

They rode in silence for a few minutes.

Then, out of nowhere, Debbie asked, "Do you have any idea how to actually siphon gas?"

"What?" Janet laughed. "That was not what I expected you to say at all. But no, I wouldn't even know where to begin."

"Me neither. Why don't you see if we can find out how it works?"

Janet used her phone to research *How to siphon gas* and found a video tutorial. She watched it while Debbie drove.

"This would be a lot more informative if I could see what the guy's doing," Debbie said.

"I'll explain once it's done," Janet promised. She watched the screen as a man used a small hand pump to get gas out of a motorcycle.

"It's basically a bike pump," she said after the video ended. "It sucks the gas up out of the gas tank and spits it out into the gas can."

"I thought it would be more sophisticated than that."

"You could use a motor if you were trying to do a lot, but you don't have to. Or you can use your mouth to suck on one end of a tube and then let it fall into a bucket."

"Wouldn't you get gas in your mouth? Isn't that dangerous?"

"I'd be worried about that too. You'd probably have to be really careful."

They arrived at Route 36 near Clasp Hollow Road, and Debbie took a right.

"So we're searching for a place by a creek, with a porch, a sycamore tree, and an RV," Debbie said.

The houses were spaced far apart, with large plots of land surrounding them. Much of the land had been cleared, so it wasn't hard to see the houses clearly. They passed a modern home, all chrome and glass and black brick, a ranch-style home, and a beautiful Victorian. There was a grouping of trailers and then a two-story colonial. But nothing that matched the description they had.

"She said it was on a corner of the creek," Janet added. "Which might make it easier—or not, I guess."

"Any idea how far down the road?" Debbie asked.

"No idea," Janet replied. "Sorry."

"You don't need to apologize. I'm impressed you remembered this much. I was right there during the conversation, and don't remember any of it."

"I think it comes from having had a teenager. You get very good at paying attention to your surroundings so you know what's going on."

They passed a brick Craftsman house, an old wooden farmhouse with a barn, and a modular home with a trampoline in the yard. After a stretch of houses, it was just farmland, waist-high corn stretching as far as the eye could see.

"It could be the other way," Janet said. "We turned right off Clasp Hollow. What if we try the other direction?"

"Let's go see what happens." Debbie made a U-turn, and they drove back past the same houses and acreage. They passed Clasp Hollow and kept going past more houses—a trailer surrounded by plastic toys, a neat wooden ranch with an immaculate garden, another Victorian, a seventies-era two-story with a basketball hoop in front.

"Those trees are so lush," Janet said, pointing toward an irregular stretch of green up ahead. "I bet there's a creek nearby."

"Well spotted."

As they drove closer, Janet saw that they were approaching a corner, and there was a large sycamore tree, its branches heavy with rich green leaves, in the yard of a large home.

"That's got to be it." Debbie slowed, and Janet saw a white wooden house with a large wraparound front porch. Behind the house was a wooden barn, and a newer RV was parked at the side of the driveway, next to a pickup truck.

"Bingo."

Debbie pulled into the driveway and slowed as they approached the side of the house. A mailbox with the name DETWEILER on it stood by the road. As Debbie switched off the engine, a woman with graying brown hair stepped out of the house. She wore yoga pants and a loose top along with sneakers, and she had a gym bag slung over her shoulder.

"Oh, hello." She smiled. "I thought it was my friend Stella pulling into the driveway. She's going to take me to our exercise class."

"Sorry," Debbie said as she and Janet climbed out of the car. "Not Stella, I'm afraid. I'm Debbie, and this is my friend Janet."

"Amanda Detweiler."

"Was gas recently stolen from your RV?" Debbie asked.

I guess we're getting right to the point, Janet thought.

"Goodness, yes. That was so upsetting." Amanda set her gym bag on the ground at her feet.

"Can you tell us what happened?" Janet asked.

"Well, like I told the police officer who came out, my husband, Dwight, and I like to go on road trips," she said. "We got the RV last year, and we've already taken it all over the place. We were going to go to Missouri to visit my sister last week, but when Dwight was getting it ready to go, he saw that the gas tank had been drained. We had half a tank when we got back from the state park on Sunday, and it was down to a quarter when he turned it on. No one had driven it, so we knew someone must have siphoned the gas. You hear about stories like that, and it's just sitting here in the yard, so I probably shouldn't be surprised."

"Are you positive about the level of the gas when you got back from the state park?" It didn't sound like a huge amount of gas. Most people probably wouldn't miss the difference between a quarter of a tank and half a tank, especially with the inaccurate level indicators in most vehicles. Or they would just assume they'd remembered wrong.

"Positive. Dwight keeps very good records. There's a little notebook inside the cab where he makes notes every time he fills the tank. He also records how many miles we go on each drive. He likes to keep track of stuff like that. It helps him watch the fuel efficiency and that kind of thing. He likes to know where every penny goes."

Dwight sounded like the kind of person who would notice missing gas.

"How much gas do you think was taken?" Janet asked.

"About fifteen gallons, give or take," Amanda said. "It's an eighty-gallon tank, so it could be a bit more or less—it's hard to say exactly— but it's enough that we knew it hadn't simply gone missing. Someone must have siphoned it off."

Filling up an eighty-gallon tank would cost a fortune. She supposed it meant they didn't have to pay for hotels when they traveled, but still.

"We figured they must have taken it at night since we're around a lot during the day. We sleep with a white noise machine, so we might not have heard if someone came into the yard while we were asleep."

Janet tried to picture how it would work. If the person had taken fifteen gallons of gas, they probably would have used three five-gallon jugs. They couldn't have carried that away on foot. They would have had to use a vehicle.

She wondered how long it would take to siphon that much gas off by hand. And why did the person need that amount? Did they really need fifteen gallons to start the fire? Was the gas thief filling up their car's gas tank as well as getting gas for the fire?

Janet was getting the sneaking suspicion that Ian was right, and this was unrelated to the warehouse case.

"You don't have a dog?" Debbie asked.

"No," Amanda said sadly. "Indy died two years ago, and Dwight can't bring himself to get another dog, though I keep telling him it would be better to have one. He was the best dog. It really would be hard to replace him."

"It's hard to say goodbye to a beloved pet," Debbie said.

"Has gas been siphoned from you before?" Janet asked.

"Once, last summer," Amanda said. "We don't know if it was the same person though. That time, I told Dwight to let it go. If someone was in that much need, I thought they were welcome to have it. But when it happened again, we knew we couldn't let it go. It can't keep happening, you know?"

"It was generous of you to let it go the first time," Janet said.

"The Lord has blessed us. It won't bankrupt us to lose a few gallons of gas. But after a while, it isn't right."

"It isn't," Janet agreed. "Do you have any idea who might have taken it?"

"Not really," Amanda said, sounding guarded.

"That's not quite the same as a no," Janet pointed out.

Amanda let out a sigh. "Dwight thinks it's a woman who lives near here. She's a little funny, to be honest. And she's stolen gas from another family nearby."

"Do you mean Jennie Ward?" Janet asked.

"You know her?"

"We've met her," Janet said. "And we'd heard that she'd stolen gas before."

"In that case, I'm sure you understand why Dwight would suspect her. But I don't know. We don't have any actual proof."

"Do you know when the theft would have occurred?" Janet asked. "I mean, aside from at night. I mean, what day?"

"That's why I called the station again this morning," Amanda said. "I originally told them it could have been taken any time after last Sunday. But when the officer was here, I was out, and Dwight told them he thought the gas must have been siphoned after last Wednesday, because that's when I went out to give it a deep clean. I always like to do that between trips. He thought I'd started the engine while I cleaned for some reason and that if the tank was low I would have noticed it. But that's his thing, and anyway, I had no reason to start it up. So I was right after all, and the gas really could have been taken any time after we got back Sunday."

If that was true, it could explain why Ian thought the timing didn't work out. Dwight had had it wrong.

"We talked about it this morning, and we realized the problem, so I called the station again this morning to let your team know. You all are so quick, though I'm sorry if they had you come in on your day off, since you're not in uniform." Amanda beamed.

Janet got a sinking feeling in her stomach. "Oh, we're not with the police."

Amanda's smile faded. "You're not?"

"No," Janet said. "I'm so sorry if we made you think that. We're merely curious about all this."

"Who are you, then?"

"We own the Whistle Stop Café," Debbie explained. "We're also kind of looking into a crime that might relate to some stolen gas. Unofficially."

"You're looking into a crime, but you're not police?" She narrowed her eyes. "What are you, private investigators?"

"Sort of," Debbie said

"Not really," Janet said at the same time.

"I'll let the police chief know we were here though," Janet added quickly.

Amanda's expression relaxed again.

A car came up the driveway, and Amanda waved at it. Stella must have arrived. "I'm sorry, but I've got to run," Amanda said.

Janet and Debbie climbed back into Debbie's car, and after they turned around and headed back to the road, Amanda hopped into Stella's car and they followed them out of the driveway.

"What did you think of that?" Debbie asked.

"I think it's sad that Jennie seems to make a habit of stealing her neighbors' gas," Janet said.

"But even if it was Jennie who siphoned gas from the RV, I don't see how that proves that she used it to set the warehouse fire," Debbie said.

"Right," Janet said. "I think there's a good chance of a connection there, but I'm not sure how to get from point A to point B."

"Neither am I."

But then, as they drove back along the country road, Janet noticed something.

Was she seeing that right?

"Debbie, pull over!"

CHAPTER TWENTY-ONE

*A*s Janet cooked dinner that night—spaghetti with meatballs and marinara sauce made from the tomatoes growing on their back porch—she thought through what Amanda had told them, what she'd seen today, and what she knew about each of the suspects.

She supposed Jedidiah Merrick had left town by now, and she imagined he was glad about that, given his experience in Dennison. The police must have cleared him and allowed him to leave.

She considered the Wilsons. Tyler's alibi had checked out, but Austin's couldn't be verified, and Janet didn't know what he'd really been up to the night of the fire. Carrie had told Janet he was at work, but he hadn't been. He'd had access to the Black Jack gum and the Crackerjack bats, which Janet was pretty sure were in the athletic bags at the Wilson home. And he had arguably the most powerful motive of all—to protect his son. He'd had the strongest reason of anyone to get rid of the evidence that would, as he saw it, ruin his son's life. Carrie had the same motivations and opportunities but seemed far less likely to Janet.

Then there was Jennie Ward. She was about to go on trial for arson, and what better way to cover up the evidence against her than to burn it all down? She'd also shown herself to be confrontational, and she had threatened Janet and Debbie. She'd stolen gas from at least one of her neighbors in the past, so it was possible that she'd stolen more and used it to set the fire. She'd been at the scene of the fire, watching the warehouse burn. She was another lead contender.

And Janet couldn't forget Todd Mills. Fraud, gross negligence, and breach of contract were serious crimes. He'd shown himself to be somewhat shifty, and he had motive to get rid of the evidence in the museum's lawsuit against him. He also chewed gum. Gum with a strange, sweet, almost anise smell that—wait. She picked up her phone and searched for *anise*, and sure enough, it was the main ingredient in licorice. She didn't know how she'd missed that before. Black Jack gum was licorice-flavored. Was that what he'd been chewing?

And then there was what she'd discovered earlier as she and Debbie drove back from the Detweilers' place...

None of the suspects had a clear way to access the police cage in the warehouse though. With Ethan off the suspect list, the idea was harder to reconcile. But thinking it through now, Janet started to wonder if the key to the cage wasn't as big an issue as she'd thought.

She finished chopping the tomatoes and added them to the pan of onions, garlic, and olive oil, and then she washed her hands and grabbed her laptop. She pulled up Todd's website again and went over the images of buildings he'd restored. Then she clicked over to his wife's social media account and scrolled through her photos until she found the one she wanted.

She opened the photo and zoomed in on something in the corner, staring at it until she was sure it was what she'd thought it was. Then she sat back in her chair and thought about the interactions she'd had with Todd over the past week and her and Debbie's visit to Patricia's office. Slowly, an idea formed.

Ian came home, bleary-eyed, and set his bag by the door.

"How did it go today?" Janet asked.

"Okay. We're narrowing in on a suspect." Ian kicked off his shoes. "It smells great in here."

"Oh?" She tried to keep her voice casual, as if she really didn't care one way or another. "Who is it?" She was sure he wasn't going to tell her, but she had to ask anyway.

Ian sighed. "Austin Wilson."

"Austin?"

She knew all the reasons Austin was a prime suspect. She knew how guilty he looked. But now that she had thought it through, she wasn't sure he was the one they should be looking at.

"I thought you would be happy to hear that," Ian said. "You were the one who brought us most of the clues that point to him. And if we get him arrested and charged this week, I can go on our family vacation after all."

That was good news.

But it wasn't good if they arrested the wrong guy.

"That's great." Janet was glad. Truly she was. But something inside her said this wasn't it, that Austin wasn't the one who had set the fire. But how could she tell Ian what she'd found without upsetting him?

The water she'd put on the stovetop earlier was boiling, so she opened a package of pasta and dumped it in.

"You don't sound very happy." Ian dried his hands on a towel. "I know Carrie is your friend, so this is hard. But with the gum wrapper and the baseball bat brand, who else could it be? So much of the evidence points to Austin."

Janet set the empty box on the counter. Everything he said was true. Austin was still a solid suspect. But it just didn't feel right.

"Do you know how he got into the warehouse?" she asked tentatively. "Or where he got the gas that was used to set the fire?"

"We're working on pinning down the method of entry," Ian said. "But it doesn't really matter where he got the gas. We have enough evidence to charge him."

For a moment, the only sounds in the kitchen were the pasta water boiling and the sauce simmering on the stove.

"Why are you suddenly changing your mind?" Ian finally asked.

"I think it might have been Todd Mills who set the fire."

"Janet, Austin doesn't have an alibi, and he has motive."

"I know. But please listen. I thought it was probably Austin too—until today. I also thought Jennie Ward was a strong suspect for a while."

"Jennie Ward almost certainly set fire to her mom's house to collect the insurance money," Ian said. "But so far we haven't been able to connect her to the warehouse fire."

"I haven't either," Janet said. "And the other people I thought might be involved don't appear to have been. Which leaves Todd. He's in a lot of trouble, legally, and he was going to lose his case. Evidence was stored in the warehouse that would have put him, if not behind bars, at least in a lot of financial trouble and ruin his business."

"Fraud on this scale is not a plausible reason to—"

"He chews Black Jack gum," Janet interrupted.

"What?"

"He's always chewing gum, and when I was talking to him last week, I smelled anise on his breath. I didn't put it together until a few minutes ago that anise is used to make Black Jack gum."

"Did he buy it from you?"

"He may have, once. Or maybe he bought it at the depot, or maybe he gets it online. I don't know. But the gum he chews definitely smells like anise. Even if he was chewing another brand of black licorice-flavored gum—and I'm not aware of any—I doubt he found one that uses anise as well. There isn't really any other gum like Black Jack. So the gum wrapper might be a connection to Todd rather than Austin."

"Chewing a unique gum is not enough reason to suspect him."

"I agree, and I wouldn't have brought it up if that was all I had to tell you. I think he knows how to pick a lock. Kim told me that a couple of weeks ago she caught him in the Pullman after he'd already turned in his key. He said that he'd gotten the key from the front desk, but Kim asked around and everyone denied giving it to him. He could have picked the lock."

That was what Patricia had been trying to tell them in her office the other day when she'd said, "I hope you're able to unlock the truth of this case." It must have come up in the course of her research for the lawsuit the museum had filed against him.

"He knows how to pick a lock, so he could have gotten into the warehouse and then into the cage without keys or signs of forced entry," she insisted. "And his son plays baseball. He has a Crackerjack bat in his house."

"What?" Ian's voice was sharp. "How do you know that? You didn't—"

"No, I didn't go to his house," Janet said. "Here." She opened her laptop again and showed Ian the photos from Dana Mills's social media.

"Have you been talking to Todd's family?" Ian asked.

"Of course not," Janet assured him. "I've just been snooping around online. I promise I haven't talked to his wife in person, and this is publicly available. Here's their son playing basketball, and this is him playing hockey, and then in this one he's playing baseball." She clicked on various photos from Dana's feed as she spoke.

"Athletic kid."

"Right. And then there's this one." She clicked on the photo of Shane in a soccer uniform in the family's foyer. It was the photo that showed the foyer full of shoes and coats and bags, in contrast to the perfectly serene photo of it that Todd had on his site. This was the one Janet had been studying earlier. "See that athletic bag on the floor?" She pointed at it. "Notice the Crackerjack logo on it?"

Ian leaned forward and squinted. "We don't know if there's a Crackerjack bat inside though."

"No, but there's a decent chance. It's not that common a brand. If he has their bag, he probably has their bat."

"It's worth checking," Ian conceded.

"Here's the other thing. You know that RV with the stolen gas?"

"I told you we followed up on that."

"I know. But apparently the woman called the station again this morning to report that her husband got the timing wrong. The gas could have been taken any time after Sunday, not just after Wednesday like he thought."

Ian watched her. "You went there to talk to them, didn't you?"

"The timing of what you told me didn't work out, so I wanted to find out why." Then, after a moment, she added, "I'm sorry. I probably shouldn't have, and I wouldn't have if I'd realized the woman had already called the station again to report the error. I don't want to get in the middle of something you're working on."

Ian raised an eyebrow at her.

Janet went on before he had the chance to verbalize what he was clearly thinking. "The thing is, I think Todd might have taken that gas."

"Why is that?"

"The RV was parked beside a house out on Route 36. I heard Veronica say that when she took the call. Do you know who lives near there?"

"Jennie Ward."

"Yes, but so does Todd Mills."

He set the empty glass on the counter. "Todd Mills lives out on Route 36?"

"In a beautiful old Victorian farmhouse, which he meticulously restored. There are pictures of it all over his web page. It's truly gorgeous, with lots of gingerbread trim alongside a ton of original woodwork. The inlaid cherry floor is so beautiful in this herringbone pattern, and there's even a stained glass window above the stairs."

"You saw all this yourself?"

"Pictures of the interior are on his website. I didn't go into his house or anything. But I did see a mailbox with 'Mills' on it as Debbie and I drove past, and that's how I noticed it at first. I saw the name and wondered. Then when I saw the house, I knew for sure it was his. It's right down the road from the place where the gas was stolen."

Ian didn't say anything. He studied her laptop, clearly processing everything she'd said.

"I'm not saying Austin didn't do it," Janet added. "He might have. I don't know. There sure are some compelling reasons to think he did. But there are also some holes in that theory—things that don't totally add up."

"Yes, they've been bothering me too."

"The Todd theory fills in those holes," she said.

"It's just a theory at this point though. We don't have enough evidence to confirm anything."

"I'm not arguing with that. All I'm saying is that I don't think Austin is necessarily your guy. Maybe he did do it. I don't have proof of anything. But I do think you should do some more digging into Todd before you arrest Austin. Better to take a few extra days and make sure you get the right guy."

Ian didn't say anything for a few more moments.

"I'll look into it," he said. "Now, is it time to eat yet? I'm starving."

CHAPTER TWENTY-TWO

Wednesday morning, Janet was ready when Patricia came in for her usual peppermint mocha. She had freshly brewed the espresso and added it to a to-go cup with steamed milk and chocolate and mint syrup, exactly as the attorney liked it. She snapped the lid on as Patricia came through the café door.

"It's the lock," Janet said. "You were telling me Todd knows how to pick a lock."

Patricia took the drink from Janet and smiled. "I can neither confirm nor deny any inferences you took from anything I said. I can't share information about one of my cases."

"What kind of punishment is Todd facing if the museum wins the lawsuit?"

"Depends on which charges stick. For breach of contract? Probably minimal consequences. But for grand theft?" Patricia shrugged. "Jail time is a distinct possibility."

"You said you weren't concerned about the fact that the evidence in the warehouse was gone," Janet said. "That's because there's more evidence somewhere else, isn't there?"

"I can neither confirm nor deny that either," Patricia replied.

"It's the Pullman, isn't it?" Janet had figured that out last night while she was trying to fall asleep. "There's still enough evidence in the Pullman to convict him, isn't there? Kim basically told us you could still see his shoddy work underneath the fixes. As long as the Pullman is around, you'll probably be able to win that case."

Patricia took a sip of her mocha. "This is really good today."

Janet took that as a yes. "What about arson? What kind of sentence would someone face if they were found guilty of that?"

"Of setting fire to a civic warehouse? Hypothetically—and this is in no way my giving professional advice—the perpetrator would probably receive quite a long prison sentence." She peered at Janet over the rim of her cup. "Let's hope they find whoever did it."

"Let's hope so," Janet echoed.

Ian had promised to investigate Todd more thoroughly. Janet didn't need to worry about finding evidence to prove that the contractor was behind the fire, no matter how certain she was.

She tried to focus on greeting their customers. Tiffany was scheduled to come by the café after she finished her shift at the pool to help Janet bake some things ahead to freeze for next week. Perhaps she'd open up more to her mom then.

Normally, Janet tried her best not to check her cell phone too much during her workday, but when it buzzed in her apron pocket as she slid a burger and fries in front of local dry cleaner Carl Miller, she took a peek after she got back to the register. She had a voice mail from Ian asking her to get in touch with him when she had a minute. She ducked into the kitchen and returned his call.

"Hi," she said when he answered. "What's going on?"

"We stopped by the hospital and talked to Austin. I know you've been upset about Carrie, so I wanted you to know what he said. He wanted me to tell you that Carrie feels awful about lying to you and

Debbie. He said she panicked and the words just came out. Austin said she'll be calling you soon and hopes you'll forgive her."

Janet felt a rush of relief along with a bit of sadness that Carrie thought she had done something Janet might not forgive her for. She decided to give her a call right after work and reassure her of her friendship.

She pulled herself back to the case. "Patricia Franklin thinks that even with the evidence in the warehouse gone, there might be enough in the Pullman itself to win the museum's lawsuit against him."

"I'll do everything I can to get him if he's the guy," Ian said. "But first we're going to focus on whether he is and finding hard evidence to back that up either way."

"Okay." Janet would pray that they found what they needed. "Good luck."

Once they closed the café for the day, Debbie left while Janet stayed behind to get ahead on her baking. She pulled out the recipes she'd gathered earlier in the week. Several of them were for muffins, which froze beautifully. Blueberry, peach crumble, and morning glory muffins would give Paulette and Debbie a good start for the week. She was sliding the second batch of muffins into the oven when Tiffany came in.

"How was the pool?" Janet asked.

"Wet." Tiffany still wore her red swimsuit beneath her white T-shirt. "Hot."

"Well at least there's AC here. Thanks for coming to help."

Tiffany nodded. "What are we making?"

"I'm finishing up the morning glory muffins."

Tiffany wrinkled her nose. "The kind no one likes?"

"Plenty of people like morning glories. We sell out every time we have them."

"Only people who want to pretend they're eating something healthy. Why not embrace that you're having a cupcake for breakfast?"

Janet laughed. "Why don't you get started on the blueberry muffins? The recipe is right there." She gestured to the card on the counter.

"Okay."

Janet had taught Tiffany to bake when she was young, and she and Tiffany had baked together countless times over the years. Doing so again brought back some of Janet's happiest memories. And it also made her think about the conversation she'd had with Debbie. She missed baking with little Tiffany so much it hurt. But she loved getting to bake with the young woman her daughter had become.

They worked together in comfortable silence for a while before Janet mustered the courage to ask, "Have you thought any more about what you want to do about the cabin?"

"Yeah. Layla and I talked about it, and we decided to skip it." Tiffany dropped a spoonful of muffin batter into one of the prepared cups. "We're going to tell Hudson we'd like to go there with him, but this wasn't what we had in mind, so maybe another time."

Janet fought back a smile. She knew Tiffany had wanted to go to the cabin. But she had also clearly been wrestling with how to stay true to her values, knowing she would feel pressure. That showed, more than anything else that had happened this summer, that Tiffany was working to make good decisions. To figure out how to navigate the more adult situations she was being faced with. To stay true to herself in the midst of external social pressure. Janet felt more than a little encouraged by that.

"That must have been a tough call to make. I know how much you wanted to go."

"I did at first. But not when I knew about the drinking and stuff. Once I heard that, I dreaded how awkward it was going to be. I realized I wouldn't be able to enjoy it at all, so there was no point in going. And Layla feels the same way. I know plenty of kids go off to college and start partying and stuff because they can, but that's not me or Layla. I'm not going to compromise what I believe in to avoid rocking the boat."

Listening to her, Janet realized that she wasn't the only one struggling to figure out the changes of this stage. She'd been so wrapped up in her own concerns about how to parent her adult daughter that she hadn't spent much time thinking about how Tiffany's other relationships were evolving and changing as they all tried to figure out who they were.

"I want to hang out with my friends but not like that," Tiffany added.

"I'm proud of you," Janet said. This competent adult side was truly beautiful to see. "I know it was a hard decision, one you didn't necessarily want to make. It's difficult to know what you want and stand up for it, even at my age. I don't know that I'd have been able to do it at yours."

"Thanks, Mom." Tiffany scooped up more batter and flicked it off the spoon and into the muffin cup. "At least we have the lake next week, right?"

"We do," Janet said. "And maybe your father will even be able to join us."

"Is he getting close to solving that fire?"

"I think he might be," Janet said.

"Thank goodness. It would be such a bummer if he didn't get to come."

Tiffany finished filling the muffin cups and slid the tray into the oven.

Two hours later, they had a large stock of goodies ready to go into the freezer for the following week. Janet surveyed the piles of muffins, scones, and cookies. They'd done well. But instead of appearing pleased, Tiffany looked confused.

"You okay?" Janet asked.

Tiffany lifted her nose and sniffed. "Do you smell that?"

"Smell what?" But even as she said it, Janet caught a whiff and knew what she was talking about. It smelled like a campfire. It smelled like—

Tiffany's voice rose in alarm. "Mom, do you smell smoke?"

CHAPTER TWENTY-THREE

J anet did smell smoke. Where was it coming from? She checked the oven, but none of the crumbly bits on the bottom had ignited. Besides, it didn't smell like toast, as an in-oven fire would have. It smelled like something was on fire.

The smoke wasn't coming from inside the kitchen. Janet burst into the café and scanned the room. The café was fine too. Whatever was burning, it wasn't coming from in there.

Tiffany ran to the window and peered out.

"Mom, there it is." She dashed to the door, and Janet followed close on her heels. They raced out onto the platform, and sure enough, smoke was coming from—

Oh no.

A thick plume of black smoke billowed up from the new Pullman.

Janet whipped out her phone and dialed 911. "Please send a fire truck to the depot immediately," she said to the dispatcher. "A Pullman sleeper car is on fire."

She couldn't see the flames, but she knew they had to be licking away at the inside of the newly restored train car. The dispatcher promised to alert the fire department and asked her to remain on the line.

Kim ran out of the depot museum, no doubt drawn by the smell of smoke as well. She shrieked and ran across the tracks and toward the train car.

"Kim, stay back!" Janet took off after her. "Is anybody inside?"

"No," Kim yelled. "The guests haven't checked in yet."

Thank goodness for that. As they got closer, the smoke got thicker, and Janet was afraid the whole car would go up.

Kim bounded up the steps and yanked open the door. Thick black smoke poured out.

"Don't go in there!" Janet cried, but Kim had already rushed inside, likely hoping to douse the flames. But as Janet reached the Pullman, something caught her eye through the open door. A red plastic gas container had been tossed onto the floor of the car.

"Kim, come out." Janet rushed up the steps after her friend and snatched the gas container from the floor. The air was so thick it hurt to breathe. She was relieved to see Kim already headed toward her, holding her T-shirt over her nose and mouth.

"It's too late," Kim said, and she and Janet hurried back down the steps and away from the train car. Once they were on the relative safety of the platform, Janet noticed movement on the far side of the car.

She saw a pair of legs and realized someone was running along the other side of the Pullman.

Only one person had a motive to set fire to the newly renovated sleeper car.

"Todd!"

The pair of legs picked up speed. Janet dropped the gas container and ran along the near side of the car, hoping to head him off at the front of the train.

She had no idea what she'd do then, but she had to stop him before he got away.

Janet pumped her legs, her lungs aching, but by the time Todd emerged from behind the train, he was so far ahead of her that there was no way she could catch him. Tiffany stood on the platform, her phone to her ear.

Off in the distance, sirens started to blare. They would be there soon. Would it be too late? Janet didn't know what to do as Todd kept running.

"Ma'am, are you still there?" the 911 operator asked. Janet had forgotten the phone was still in her hand.

Janet put the phone to her ear. "Yes. I'm here. Please hurry!" She continued down the platform, and as she got closer to Tiffany, she heard snatches of what Tiffany was saying and realized who she was talking to.

"He's headed east, Dad." Tiffany shouted to be heard over the chaos around her. "He's running along the train tracks. Where are you guys?" After a pause, she said, "He's on the other side of the depot. If you take the alleyway, you could cut him off."

Tiffany was telling Ian where Todd was headed. Somehow, even in all the fear and excitement, she had kept a level head and thought to call her dad.

"I can hear your sirens now. You're getting close," Tiffany said.

Todd was still running down the train tracks, away from the burning train car, away from them. How far did he think he would get on foot? Did he really think he could escape? Then again, given what he'd been up to lately, he didn't seem to be operating on logic so much as panic.

Sirens blared, and a police cruiser roared up. Before Janet knew what was happening, Ian was out of the car and running after Todd, Brendan a step behind him and gaining ground. As they watched, Brendan sprinted ahead of Ian and launched himself toward Todd. Janet and Tiffany both gasped, and Janet felt her stomach drop. He couldn't possibly reach Todd from that distance.

But then Brendan connected with Todd, knocking him to the ground. Was the deputy okay? That was a hard fall.

But Brendan didn't seem rattled by it at all. He pinned Todd to the ground, despite the guilty man's efforts to get away. Somehow, Brendan managed to keep the contractor down long enough for Ian to slap handcuffs on his wrists. Janet let out a breath she hadn't realized she'd been holding.

It was over. Todd Mills was in custody.

Janet spun around and saw fire trucks spraying water at the Pullman. There would be damage, both from the fire and the water they used to put it out, but hopefully the Pullman could be saved and the evidence against Todd intact enough to be used in court.

Best of all, any doubt they'd had about who was behind the warehouse fire was put to rest. Janet didn't know how long Todd would spend behind bars, but she hoped, for the sake of his family that he would be able to turn his life around by the time he got out.

Brendan shoved Todd into the back seat of the cruiser, but Ian didn't seem to be in a huge hurry to get him to the station. He stood with his arm around Tiffany, watching the water from the fire department hoses beat the flames down. Janet walked over to them, and he put his other arm over her shoulders. They stood there together, watching until the flames died out completely.

CHAPTER TWENTY-FOUR

Janet had spoken to Brendan, Ian, and Mike Gleason multiple times over the course of the past few hours. She explained how Tiffany had smelled the smoke first and how they'd run out and found the Pullman in flames. She told them how she'd pulled the gas can—likely the same one that had been used to carry the gas that started the warehouse fire—from the car and how she'd recognized Todd and called 911 while Tiffany called Ian.

Kim had told the officers her version of the story, how she'd also smelled the smoke and come running, and Tiffany had talked to them as well.

Ian had explained that he and Brendan had actually been on their way to the depot to warn Kim that there was a chance Todd would try to set fire to the Pullman. He also explained that his visit to Todd's house that afternoon seemed to have spooked the contractor.

"He realized we were onto him," Ian said to everyone who was gathered in the briefing room.

"I think he honestly thought he was going to get away with it up to that point," Brendan said. The deputy had bandages on his right arm and an ice pack on his left knee, but he was in good spirits.

"But how did he know there was evidence inside the train car that could be used against him?" Janet asked. "Patricia wouldn't confirm it to me, so I'm positive she wouldn't have told him."

"I'm afraid that's my fault," Kim said. "He was hanging around the depot museum this morning when I came in. He was demanding payment again. I'm not sure why he thought I would pay him when we had an active lawsuit against him, but I lost my cool and told him that even if the evidence in the warehouse was gone, we still had plenty in the new Pullman to prove he was a crook." Kim folded her arms across her chest. "I suppose that's when he realized he needed to get rid of that evidence as well."

"And he must have realized the clock was ticking when we showed up to ask him about the warehouse fire," Brendan said.

"But why would he think setting the Pullman on fire would help him?" Janet asked. "I get that he was trying to destroy the evidence, but he already knew the police were on his trail. Now he's facing two charges of arson instead of one. Didn't he realize he would simply make things worse for himself?"

"I don't get the sense that a lot of thought was put into it," Ian said. "When we spoke with him today, he reminded me of an animal caught in a trap. Lashing out at everything because he was desperate to get free."

"I think he knew he was pretty much out of options," Brendan added.

"The suspect did admit that he knew the car was between guests, so he was pretty sure no one would be inside," Ian said. "Which I guess shows a bit of humanity. He didn't want anyone to get hurt."

"He has a funny way of showing it," Brendan said, rubbing his knee.

Despite the tense situation, Janet had to laugh. "You knocked him over pretty hard, you know."

"The suspect will be fine," Ian said with a smile. "All Vaughn's time in the gym has finally paid off."

Brendan chuckled.

"Okay, so now we know it was Todd who set the warehouse fire," Janet said. "And we know he picked the locks to get in. But what about Austin? How did he know about the fire starting in the evidence cage?"

"Meyers," Brendan said with a grimace. "The kid has some things to learn yet."

"Unfortunately, one of the officers who questioned him let that slip," Ian explained with a frown at Brendan. "I followed up with Austin after you told me about what he'd said to you, and it seems Officer Meyers's questions about his whereabouts on the night of the fire allowed him to put two and two together."

"Oh dear."

"I was there with him," Brendan said. "I tried to rein him in, but he wasn't exactly good at framing his questions."

"Meyers is young," Ian said with a sigh. "I'll work with him on how to interrogate a suspect. He'll be a good officer once he's had more training."

Janet processed this. So Ethan Meyers hadn't taken money to pass along the key to the cage, but he had been responsible for tipping off a suspect that the cage was important. That wasn't a great start to his career, but she knew Ian would be patient with him. They had all been inexperienced once.

"What about the gas?" Janet said. "It was Todd who took the gas from the neighbor's RV, right? Why did he take so much? Surely he didn't need as much as he took, did he?"

"Gas is expensive," Brendan said with a shrug. "It sounded like he wanted to get some gas without being seen buying it, but he took a lot while he was at it. Might as well fill up your car, right?"

After a few more questions, the officers dismissed Kim, Janet, and Tiffany. Ian promised he'd be home as soon as he could.

Janet slung her arm around Tiffany's shoulders as they walked out of the police station. "It was really smart of you to call your dad and tell him exactly where Todd was."

Tiffany shrugged. "I took a shot in the dark that he'd be close enough to do something about it. I didn't know he would be, but at least he'd have a direction to start his search for the guy."

They walked down the stairs and out onto the street. Outside, the evening air was warm and still, and the first stars started to emerge in the sky.

"You have a lot of sense," Janet said. "And you've shown that this week. Not just with the phone call but also with the whole cabin thing. You've shown me that you're using good judgment, and that makes me so proud."

Tiffany smiled at her. "I know it's been hard for you, Mom, and I appreciate that you've given me the freedom to make my own decisions. I know you still want to tell me what to do all the time, but I appreciate that you don't."

Janet laughed. "I don't want to tell you what to do *all* the time."

"Just most of the time." Tiffany laughed. "But really. You've done a great job, Mom. I'm doing all right. I'll always need your wisdom and guidance, and I'm grateful when I get it, but I'm going to be fine."

"You're more than all right, but your dad and I will always be there to bail you out if you need help. Or, in your dad's case, to show up in a police car and handcuff the bad guy."

"It is kind of cool having a cop for a dad," Tiffany admitted.

"I love you, Tiff." Janet pulled her in for a hug.

"I love you too, Mom."

The stars spread out in a tapestry above them against the darkening sky. For a moment, neither of them spoke. They gazed up at the sky, taking it all in.

Janet reminded herself to treasure this moment. To commit to memory the feeling of her daughter beside her for as long she could. Summer wouldn't last forever. Soon, Tiffany would return to college, and then, eventually, to her own adult life. They wouldn't always have their daughter staying with them.

And that meant they'd done their job. The goal was to launch children out into the world, to see them grow into responsible adults with their own lives.

She wasn't sure she was ready. She didn't want to say goodbye to the child she loved.

But watching Tiffany enjoy a clear summer night sky, Janet realized that her daughter had turned out pretty great. The next few years would bring enormous changes. But God was unchanging, and He would see them through this. Tiffany was up to the challenge—they all were. Tiffany was in the process of leaving behind her childhood and figuring out who she was going to be. It was an exciting time, and based on what she'd seen so far, Tiffany was going to be someone pretty spectacular.

Janet couldn't wait to see it.

Dear Reader,

The idea for this story, like so many of them, came from real life. A few months before I wrote this, there was a big fire at a warehouse in Brooklyn, New York, not far from where I live. When it came out that the warehouse was a police evidence storage facility, it didn't take long for the speculation to start. Naturally, my friends and I assumed the fire was set by someone hoping to destroy the evidence of their crimes. I'm not a police officer, and it's a good thing, because it turned out the fire was started by an electrical short and wasn't suspicious in the slightest. But the idea of someone setting fire to police evidence to cover up a crime captured my attention, and this story is the result.

The American Soldiers Homecoming Tribute Festival featured in this story is a real festival that used to be an annual event at the Dennison Depot. I took a lot of liberties with it in this story, but it was fun to incorporate a real event into the book. I am so inspired by how the real team at the depot honors our soldiers, past and present.

The subplot for this story—about Janet struggling to understand how to parent Tiffany now that she's back from college—came about kind of accidentally. I initially intended to write about Janet's stress as she prepped for her vacation, but the story that came out wasn't about that at all but about a mother wrestling with complicated feelings about her daughter growing up. Once it was on the page, it became clear to me what was going on.

While I was writing this story, my older daughter said goodbye to the school she's attended since kindergarten. In the fall, she will move to a new junior high/high school combination, where she'll be in seventh grade. She'll be taking the subway to school on her own and will be in school with kids several years and many levels of experience older. I know things are about to change for her and for us in big ways.

As she baked brownies for all her former teachers and said goodbye to the friends from her elementary-school years, I realized that we only have a few years left before she'll be leaving for college and moving out for good. I feel her childhood slipping through my fingers, and I'm not sure how our relationship will change as she becomes more independent in the coming years. I think I was working through that as I was writing this story, and all the fear and angst I was feeling ended up on the page. I hope what comes through—and what I hope is true in real life—is that our children will understand that a mother's love never changes, and that God, who is the same yesterday, today, and forever, is our rock and our stronghold in the midst of it all.

I hope you enjoyed reading this story as much as I enjoyed writing it.

Best,
Beth Adams

ABOUT the AUTHOR

Beth Adams lives in Brooklyn, New York, with her husband and two daughters. When she's not writing, she's trying to find time to read mysteries.

TRUTH BEHIND the FICTION

I knew I wanted to incorporate the Pullman sleeper car into a story as soon as I saw that you really could sleep in a restored car at the Dennison Depot. It must be such a unique experience to stay in a restored train car, and while I haven't had the chance to do so myself, it sure seems like the owners have restored the historic car to the highest standard. The old cars hearken back to the golden age of train travel, with private compartments, pull-down beds, and space to spread out for a cross-country journey. By the way, the shady contractor and his shoddy work are completely made up, as is the fire at the end that damages the car, so you can expect nothing but the finest at the actual depot. If you ever make it to Dennison, please check it out!

FROM the HOME-FRONT KITCHEN

Janet's Kabobs

These kabobs are perfect for when it's too hot to turn on the oven, and they are endlessly adaptable, so you can use whatever ingredients you have on hand. Here's the recipe Janet used, but feel free to substitute any fresh veggies or meat you like. Adjust cooking times accordingly to make sure the meat is thoroughly cooked.

Ingredients:

For the marinade:

¼ cup olive oil

¼ cup soy sauce

¼ cup honey

2 teaspoons minced garlic

Salt and pepper to taste

For the skewers:

1 pound boneless skinless chicken, cut into 1-inch pieces

½ pound Halloumi cheese (or any grilling cheese)

2 bell papers, chopped into 1-inch pieces

½ red onion, chopped into 1-inch pieces

1 pint cherry tomatoes

½ pound mushrooms

Directions:

If using wooden skewers, soak in water for half an hour before assembling kabobs.

Mix marinade ingredients together in small bowl.

Thread vegetables, chicken, and cheese onto skewers in whatever order you choose. Set the skewers into shallow baking pan.

Pour marinade over skewers, turning to coat.

Let sit for at least half an hour, rotating to make sure everything soaks in marinade.

When you're ready to cook, heat the grill to medium-high heat and cook 5 to 7 minutes on each side, or until chicken is cooked through.

Serve over rice or whatever grain you have handy.

Read on for a sneak peek of another exciting book in the Whistle Stop Café Mysteries *series!*

WHEN YOU WISH UPON A STAR

BY BECKY MELBY

Dennison, Ohio
May 28, 1942

"Summer!"

Roxanne Britton practically squealed the word to her best friend, Caroline Davis. They had just stopped in front of Roxy's house, waving goodbye to Minnie Franklin, who continued to walk home.

"Shorts," Caroline agreed, clutching a handful of her plaid skirt. "Can't wait to be done with slips and stockings."

After tugging her damp blouse away from her skin, Roxy pulled a key from her purse. "I'm going to get the mail and grab some cooler clothes."

"Okay. Mom said she'd have a special treat for the last day of school, so hurry."

"I'll be there in a jiffy." She trotted up the sidewalk then paused and called back, "Hey. We're officially juniors."

"Upperclasswomen." Caroline held out her stack of class notebooks. "If it wasn't so hot, I'd say we should make a bonfire with these."

"Sounds like a good idea for a Friday night party at the camp."

Her suggestion was met with an arch of a perfectly plucked brow. "Wouldn't that be a gas? Let's talk to the gang and see if we can pull it off."

"It's going to be a clear night. We could work on our Star Finder badges."

"Great idea. Go change. We plan better in bare feet."

"Agreed." Roxy bounded up the steps to her front porch. The black metal mailbox squeaked as she opened it. Inside, she found two bills, a week-old copy of the Hollywood Citizen-News, LIFE *magazine, and a letter from Jade.*

She glanced at the return address. Jade Tanaka, still at the same address, the adobe house near Wilton and Monroe in Los Angeles.

Not a detention camp.

She breathed a sigh of relief but then noticed with surprise that the letter was addressed to Mrs. Eric Britton. Not to Roxy but to her mother.

Folding the mail with the letter on top, she tucked it under one arm and unlocked the front door. As she kicked off her loafers, the silence in the stuffy, dark interior caused a hitch in her breathing, the way it always did.

Eight weeks ago—before her mother had been asked to serve a three-month stint at Walter Reed General Hospital in Washington, DC, with the US Army Nurse Corps—there would have been music playing on the pho-nograph when Roxy walked in from school. Her mother would have been singing "Tumbling Tumbleweeds" or "Empty Saddles" along with Bing Crosby while cleaning, baking, or painting another watercolor landscape.

Six months ago, her father would have been at his drafting table in the room to her right, the one with the beveled glass door, designing homes for clients throughout east central Ohio. Not on a ship some-where in the Pacific.

But six months ago, the country had not been at war.

Staying with Caroline, her next-door neighbor and best friend since fifth grade, had sounded exciting when her mother and Caroline's had first proposed the idea of Roxy and her little sister, Diana, moving in with the Davises. But three months was feeling much, much longer than she'd anticipated.

Caroline's mother, one of the kindest women she knew, had been her second mom for years, but she'd never been fond of Mr. Davis, whose arbitrary rules were unreasonable and controlling. And the man was as narrow-minded as a person could be. She tried not to judge him too harshly. Caroline's brother, Steven, was stationed in France. That was Mr. Davis's reason for distrusting anyone with a German-sounding name. But Roxy's father was somewhere in the Pacific, fighting the Japanese, and that didn't make Roxy prejudiced against Japanese people.

Still—as she reminded herself every morning when he demanded the girls finish every bite on their breakfast plates—cooperating with his rules so that her parents needn't worry while they served was one small part she could play in the war effort.

Upstairs in her room, Roxy opened her bottom dresser drawer and pulled out the two pairs of shorts *she owned. From the closet, she grabbed a short sailor jumpsuit, two lightweight dresses, and a couple of sleeveless blouses. "Bring on summer," she said out loud. Her words echoed strangely in the empty house.*

She slipped out of her A-line skirt, full slip, and plaid blouse. She'd heeded the call for nylon stockings that could be used for making ropes and parachutes, resigning herself to wearing socks instead. She had kept a single pair of nylons tucked away for special occasions.

After putting on a shirt with navy and white stripes and a pair of baby-blue cotton shorts that belted at the waist, she perched on the bed and slid a letter opener under the flap of the letter from Jade.

Dear Aunt Lu,

In your Christmas letter, you said we were all welcome to come and stay with you if the need arose. Well, Mother and Father have been forced to move. I intended to go with them, but Father was so heartbroken at the thought of abandoning his work that I have decided to defy the order and continue his translations. I am leaving tonight and praying with every mile that I can get to you. I apologize for this short notice. I have tried calling you several times but haven't caught you at home. If it won't work for me to stay with you for any reason at all, I understand.

I would never want to put you and your family in a dangerous situation.

By the time you read this, I will be on my way. Again, please know I will understand if this doesn't work.

I pray for you, Roxy, Diana, and Uncle Eric daily. It will be wonderful to put my arms around you and catch up, even if it's for a short visit. I look forward to joining you for the Sunday church service you've told us about.

All my love,

Jade

The letter had been postmarked three days before. Jade could drive. Had she taken the family car? Or would she be arriving by train?

Roxy's heart began to pound in her chest. Jade was like a sister. They'd been raised together until five years ago. She would never turn Jade away. Could her dear friend stay here in the unoccupied house, hiding like a fugitive?

One thing was certain. She would not be welcome in Mr. Davis's home. Roxy would have to come up with something else. And for Jade, she would.

The August air was already thick and muggy on Friday morning when Debbie Albright arrived at the Whistle Stop Café, which she and her best friend, Janet Shaw, had owned for more than a year. As she walked through the door, she was startled to see Janet behind the counter, hands on her hips, in a stance that reminded Debbie of an agitated referee.

"What's wrong?" Debbie gaped at her friend. In more than thirty years of friendship, she'd rarely seen Janet so visibly angry.

"This." Janet pushed her phone across the counter.

On the screen was their first one-star review. Her heart sank. They'd always received enthusiastic comments about their food and service. Earlier in the week, a tourist visiting Dennison for the first time had written, *The food and friendliness in this nostalgic café housed in a historic Ohio train depot lives up to the town's claim to be 'A great place to call home.' Even if you, like my wife and I, are only passing through, you'll walk away feeling like you've spent an hour with family.*

"Read it." Janet swatted at a bit of flour on the front of her T-shirt featuring the words Let's Dough This! printed under a picture of a rolling pin.

Debbie held the phone closer and read the acerbic words out loud.

"'Never have I received such poor service. I must have sat for half an hour waiting for someone to take my order and then another half an hour to receive my food. With all the hype I've read about this place, I expected something more than what you can get at any

Midwest greasy spoon.'" Debbie felt her anger building as she read the final sentence. "'The depot museum was worth a drive, but don't waste your time at the café.'" She glanced up, knowing her expression likely mirrored Janet's. "'Greasy spoon'? And no one has *ever* had to wait half an hour to have their order taken."

"I know that, you know that, and our regulars know that. But what will this say to people who've never been here and find us online?"

"Who wrote this?" Debbie squinted at the small letters. "Gastro Gnome?" She inhaled sharply. "That lady—I think it was Tuesday. She wore a shirt that said 'Gastro Gnome.'"

"Now that you say that, I remember commenting on the cute gnome on her shirt," Janet said. "Pretty sure she didn't smile once, and I know she didn't tip."

"She told me she'd recently moved here with her son and his family. I got the impression she wasn't happy about the move."

"She lives here?" Janet grimaced. A timer went off behind her. "Time to fry doughnuts. We can't let this derail us."

Debbie rolled her eyes. "Save your railroad jokes for the customers. Ah, like this one."

Harry Franklin—followed closely by his black-and-white canine sidekick, Crosby—shuffled to his usual seat in front of the window then mopped his brow with a handkerchief. "In this heat, you can shut off your fryer and cook directly on the rails. Back in the day, I saw plenty of people down on their luck doing that."

Debbie smiled at the ninety-six-year-old, still handsome African-American who had come to the depot every morning for more than eighty years. Starting out as a porter in his teens, he'd gone on to be a conductor after World War II. Now, thirty years after retiring, he still came daily to eat breakfast and watch the trains. He would be a good one to sic on Gastro Gnome and set her straight.

Debbie pressed her lips together, holding back a laugh. "Makes a person count their blessings, doesn't it?" She set a glass of ice water in front of him. "Can I talk you into an iced coffee this morning?"

Harry's lined face scrunched. "I usually wouldn't say you can call it coffee once you pour it over ice, but I'm going to make an exception this morning. Patricia, crazy girl that she is, will want hers hot. What's in the bakery case today?" His granddaughter, local attorney Patricia Franklin, often joined him for breakfast.

"Janet made some puff pastry tarts with cream cheese and fresh fruit. Cool and light."

"We'll take two. I mean three." Harry winked. "Don't tell Patricia about the third one."

The bell above the door jingled, and Harry's granddaughter came in, chatting with another frequent customer. Ashling Kelly's long auburn hair was braided and coiled around her head like a crown. She wore a bright red T-shirt that said JILL OF ALL TRADES and walked with a slight limp most people wouldn't even notice, all that remained from a car accident nearly a year before. She waved at Debbie and took a seat at the counter.

"Morning, Ashling." Debbie stepped around the end of the counter and filled two glasses with ice. "The usual?"

"Yes, please. And when you and Janet have a minute, I want to ask you something."

After serving Harry and Patricia, Debbie set a chocolate-frosted doughnut and an iced coffee, heavy on the cream and sugar, in front of Ashling. She poked her head into the kitchen and called to Janet, who finished assembling an ice cream sandwich with giant chocolate chip cookies and popped it into the freezer on her way to the front. It was National Ice Cream Sandwich Day, and they were prepared to help the lunch crowd celebrate.

Ashling took a slurp of her drink then pulled a stack of brightly colored flyers from a canvas bag. "Would you mind posting a couple of these?"

Debbie examined the papers. Below an image of a magnifying glass were the words, *Looking for girls in grades 9–12 who want to make friends and make a difference!* The remainder of the text announced an informational Girl Scout meeting to be held in the high school cafeteria on August 7.

The last line on the page brought a smile to Debbie's face.

Questions? Contact Ashling Kelly, leader.

Janet's expression reflected the delight Debbie felt. Her daughter, Tiffany, had always been close with Ashling. "When did you become a leader?"

"Yesterday." Ashling practically vibrated with enthusiasm. "I mean, it was official yesterday. I enrolled in an online training class last month. I'm taking over for the current leader, who's due to have a baby any day."

"How wonderful," Debbie said. "Is it a big job?"

"Yes and no. There are only five girls in the troop now, and I'm hoping to grow it. That's where the work will come in. I'm fully aware that some parents might not feel confident with such a young leader, so I'm turning to the seasoned, experienced, wise, confident women who have guided my life's journey. I beg them to come alongside me and impart wisdom to young, impressionable girls." As if the over-the-top words were not enough, she accompanied them with puppy-dog eyes and hands pressed together in a comically pleading gesture.

Janet laughed. "Has anyone ever said no to you?"

Ashling rested one fingertip on her chin. "Not that I can recall."

Debbie rolled her eyes. "How are we supposed to refuse after that?"

"You're not." Ashling lifted her cup and took a sip, her rosy, freckled cheeks plumping as she smiled around her straw. "Seriously, you two were the first people I thought of. You've both been such amazing encouragers this past year. I want to be that for girls who don't already have cheerleaders in their lives."

Debbie was surprised by the unexpected tightening of her throat. It had been a challenging year for Ashling. Eight months ago, she'd been in an accident that had left her with a concussion and a broken leg, plus totaled the pickup truck she used for her business, Jill of All Trades. To look at her now, with the sun-kissed glow on her face, it was hard to believe she'd been in an induced coma in December, her skin almost as white as the sheets she lay on.

"How can we help?" Janet asked.

"Grandma has such cool stories of scouting when she was a girl. I want to teach the girls some old-school skills."

"I see why you came to us." Debbie made her voice wobble like someone twice her age. "You want someone who remembers life in the Dark Ages, before every kid had a cell phone and laptop. Well, you came to the right people. We were Girl Scouts in the old days when kids played outside, riding bikes and roller skating. We had one computer in the house, and it was dial-up." She gasped in mock horror.

"And if we wanted to watch a movie, we had to go the store and rent a VHS tape." Janet sighed and pressed the back of her hand to her forehead. "You have no idea how rough we old folks had it."

Ashling laughed. "I didn't mean—well, yes, I guess that's exactly what I meant. Minus the 'old' part. I want to draw on the experiences of people of *all* ages, especially former scouts. Like Girl Scouting through the ages."

Janet rested her fingertips on Ashling's hand. "Love it. You know we'll do anything we can to help you. I'd be happy to teach some baking skills."

Debbie chewed on her bottom lip. From the time she'd graduated college until less than two years before, her life had been consumed with a demanding corporate job in Cleveland and hanging out with friends in her limited free time. Other than reading and journaling, she'd never taken the time to develop any more hobbies.

Unless compiling stories of Dennison's Greatest Generation residents counted. "I could talk to the girls about journaling and preserving family histories."

Ashling beamed. "That would be wonderful. Thank you both. I knew I could count on you." She glanced at her watch then pointed to her untouched doughnut. "Can I take this to go? I've been talking and forgetting to eat. I have to be at a job in ten minutes, but I'll be back tomorrow. I'm grateful for any ideas you can come up with."

After Ashling left, Debbie turned to Janet. "Earlier this year, Kim had a Girl Scout display over in the museum. It was all about the scouts who volunteered during the war. Bet there'd be some interesting things in that collection if she still has it. I think it would help prospective scouts feel connected to the organization."

"That's right. She had a bunch of photographs and a couple of uniforms from the forties."

"And a handbook. It was displayed in the glass case. It's probably full of exactly the kind of nostalgic stuff Ashling wants to explain the organization through the ages." Debbie swept the café with her gaze. It wasn't a busy morning, but she wasn't sure she could bring herself to abandon Janet in case there was a rush.

"Go ask her." Janet laughed. "You'll be useless here until you find out if she still has it."

Debbie nudged her best friend with her shoulder. "Thanks. I'll be back in a jiffy."

"It's in a white library box. I know I labeled it. It's around here somewhere." Kim Smith, curator of the Dennison Depot Museum, brushed dark, feathery bangs away from her face as she scanned the contents of the small storeroom.

The room was not air-conditioned, and even after a couple minutes of searching, Debbie started to feel claustrophobic. She scanned shelves marked with labels like Vintage Christmas, Salvation Army Brochures, and Letters from Home. Then she spotted it on a top shelf, a white box marked Girl Scouts WWII. "Found it." She pulled a step stool close then, climbed up, slid the box out, and handed it down to Kim.

"Good work. Let's get out of this oven," Kim said. "Take the whole box. I won't need it for a while, so I'm glad it'll be put to good use in the meantime."

Back in the café, Janet passed Debbie with two plates of bacon, eggs, and hash browns balanced on her forearm and a coffeepot in her free hand. Debbie set the box on the counter and lifted the lid. "I'm just going to make sure the book is in here. That's all. Then I'm back to work."

"Sure you are. Don't worry about me. I can do it. All by myself."

Ignoring Janet's exaggerated sigh, Debbie examined the box's contents. Plastic zipper bags contained uniforms beside a stack of notebooks. When she lifted one, she saw the green spine of a cloth-covered book. It was the handbook she'd been hunting for.

"Hey, I've got a bit of history for you."

Debbie smiled as Harry approached, arm in arm with his stylish granddaughter. She'd heard many of his stories dozens of times, but every once in a while a new one popped up. "What's that, Harry?"

He indicated the box. "My cousin Minnie was the first African American Girl Scout in Dennison. Must have been 1940 or so when she joined up."

Debbie had a vague recollection of meeting Minnie somewhere years ago. She rested a hand on Harry's forearm. "Ashling would love to hear that. She became a scout leader yesterday."

"Tell her I'm willing to pass on any questions. Minnie is always happy to pass on her wisdom." Harry saluted her with his to-go cup and walked toward the door with Patricia, Crosby at his heels. The group paused to talk to the next person walking through the door.

Debbie opened the front cover of the green handbook.

Happy 15th Birthday, Roxanne!
Hope the next few years of Girl Scouting are wonderful. We are so
proud of the kind and generous young woman you are becoming.

Love you so much, Mom and Dad
September 3, 1941

Across from the copyright page, which showed that the book had been printed in April of 1941, was a page with blanks filled in with dark blue ink.

THIS IS MY BOOK
DATE: September 3, 1941
TROOP: No. 52
NAME: Roxanne Britton
ADDRESS: 626 Grant St., Dennison, Ohio

As she turned another page, something fell out and drifted to the floor. A pressed flower. She bent to pick it up.

"Don't!" Harry's black leather shoe blocked her way. "Don't touch that, Debbie. It's monkshood. Also known as wolfsbane or aconite. It's deadly. Just touching it could kill you."

While you are waiting for the next fascinating story in the Whistle Stop Café Mysteries, check out another Guideposts mystery series!

SAVANNAH SECRETS

Welcome to Savannah, Georgia, a picture-perfect Southern city known for its manicured parks, moss-covered oaks, and antebellum architecture. Walk down one of the cobblestone streets, and you'll come upon Magnolia Investigations. It is here where two friends have joined forces to unravel some of Savannah's deepest secrets. Tag along as clues are exposed, red herrings discarded, and thrilling surprises revealed. Find inspiration in the special bond between Meredith Bellefontaine and Julia Foley. Cheer the friends on as they listen to their hearts and rely on their faith to solve each new case that comes their way.

The Hidden Gate
A Fallen Petal
Double Trouble
Whispering Bells
Where Time Stood Still
The Weight of Years
Willful Transgressions

Season's Meetings
Southern Fried Secrets
The Greatest of These
Patterns of Deception
The Waving Girl
Beneath a Dragon Moon
Garden Variety Crimes
Meant for Good
A Bone to Pick
Honeybees & Legacies
True Grits
Sapphire Secret
Jingle Bell Heist
Buried Secrets
A Puzzle of Pearls
Facing the Facts
Resurrecting Trouble
Forever and a Day

A NOTE FROM the EDITORS

We hope you enjoyed another exciting volume in the Whistle Stop Café Mysteries series, published by Guideposts. For over seventy-five years, Guideposts, a nonprofit organization, has been driven by a vision of a world filled with hope. We aspire to be the voice of a trusted friend, a friend who makes you feel more hopeful and connected.

By making a purchase from Guideposts, you join our community in touching millions of lives, inspiring them to believe that all things are possible through faith, hope, and prayer. Your continued support allows us to provide uplifting resources to those in need. Whether through our communities, websites, apps, or publications, we inspire our audiences, bring them together, and comfort, uplift, entertain, and guide them. Visit us at guideposts.org to learn more.

We would love to hear from you. Write us at Guideposts, P.O. Box 5815, Harlan, Iowa 51593 or call us at (800) 932-2145. Did you love *Set the World on Fire*? Leave a review for this product on guideposts .org/shop. Your feedback helps others in our community find relevant products.

Find inspiration, find faith, find Guideposts.

Shop our best sellers and favorites at
guideposts.org/shop

Or scan the QR code to go directly to our Shop

Find more inspiring stories in these best-loved Guideposts fiction series!

Mysteries of Lancaster County

Follow the Classen sisters as they unravel clues and uncover hidden secrets in Mysteries of Lancaster County. As you get to know these women and their friends, you'll see how God brings each of them together for a fresh start in life.

Secrets of Wayfarers Inn

Retired schoolteachers find themselves owners of an old warehouse-turned-inn that is filled with hidden passages, buried secrets, and stunning surprises that will set them on a course to puzzling mysteries from the Underground Railroad.

Tearoom Mysteries Series

Mix one stately Victorian home, a charming lakeside town in Maine, and two adventurous cousins with a passion for tea and hospitality. Add a large scoop of intriguing mystery, and sprinkle generously with faith, family, and friends, and you have the recipe for *Tearoom Mysteries*.

Ordinary Women of the Bible

Richly imagined stories—based on facts from the Bible—have all the plot twists and suspense of a great mystery, while bringing you fascinating insights on what it was like to be a woman living in the ancient world.

To learn more about these books, visit Guideposts.org/Shop